C000153942

Is this for Real?

ANNIE BROWN

AuthorHouse™ UK
1663 Liberty Drive
Bloomington, IN 47403 USA
www.authorhouse.co.uk
Phone: UK TFN: 0800 0148641 (Toll Free inside the UK)
*   UK Local: (02) 0369 56322 (+44 20 3695 6322 from outside the UK)*

© 2023 Annie Brown. All rights reserved.

No part of this book may be reproduced, stored in a retrieval system, or
transmitted by any means without the written permission of the author.

Published by AuthorHouse 06/12/2023

ISBN: 978-1-7283-5516-0 (sc)
ISBN: 978-1-7283-5515-3 (e)

Print information available on the last page.

Any people depicted in stock imagery provided by Getty Images are models,
and such images are being used for illustrative purposes only.
Certain stock imagery © Getty Images.

This book is printed on acid-free paper.

Because of the dynamic nature of the Internet, any web addresses or
links contained in this book may have changed since publication and
may no longer be valid. The views expressed in this work are solely those
of the author and do not necessarily reflect the views of the publisher,
and the publisher hereby disclaims any responsibility for them.

Acknowledgements

I would like to dedicate this book to my daughter, Helena and my son, Paul and thank them so much for listening to all my stories over and over again. Your patience has been incredible, thank you.

This book is also in memory of my dear friend, Tessa Gilling who sadly passed away far too soon.

She came to my help when I was at my lowest at school and showed me a love I had never felt before. Despite the adversity I gave her, she stood firm and loved me.

I know you are with our heavenly Father and we will meet again.

Introduction

I wrote my story down as a step to put behind what needs to rest.

It enabled my mind to be clear of clutter and be free and it really helped. I can wholly recommend writing a book as every one of us has a story and it has been better than any therapy.

Abuse – emotional, physical, sexual or spiritual brings the victim to always ask themselves, is this for real? Often times because the perpetrator says it isn't.

I hope as you read this book it causes you to gasp, giggle and also wonder how on earth this fiery, outrageously adventurous young girl that is smothered by emotional turmoil, bounces back.

She never ever allowed the inner fight to completely be dashed and with a divine intervention – conquered.

Why – "Is this for Real?"

I was pondering what to call my story. A close friend of mine noticed that every time I mentioned or recalled an event, the innermost struggle I had, and kept repeating with tears streaming down my cheeks, was .... Is this for real?

The penny dropped and I realised that this had been the aching in my heart to know.

Vivid memories, spiritual encounters, and childhood recollections to me are real. They can be present despite happening many years ago as memories seem to have no time attached to them.

I realised for my own sanity and those I listen to who have similar experiences – that reality, to make sense out of life's events, is vital for well-being and can be impossible or seem impossible to accomplish in a world of grey and confusion.

I needed to experience and know the truth. I have spent so many years seeking this. Unless the truth was known, I had no peace.

I came to the conclusion that it didn't matter whether this story is real to others because it is real to me. God knows and I can rest on that. The struggle of emotional pain has ceased.

The knowledge of being and knowing we are loved, I believe, gives us a peace that no one can take away.

In the Bible, there is a verse in the book of John Chapter 14 verse 27 which I adore, it is:-

"Peace, I leave with you; My peace, I give to you, not as the world gives, give I to you. Let not your heart be troubled nor afraid (dismayed)."

Chapter 1

BRISTOL – NOVEMBER 1964

"Four local students had managed to gain access to the stage lighting gantries, and they tipped bags of flour onto the Beatles' heads!"

John and his gang could not believe how successful their stunt was and the adrenaline was pulsating through their bodies ten to the dozen as they fled from the scene.

They had meticulously plotted the perfect location for their prank, which was to be directly above where the band would be playing, hiding beside the stage lighting gantries. They had planned this many months in advance and frequently visited the site where the Beatles would perform. It was an excellent place as the emergency exit consisted of one long metal ladder on the outside of the building. This was to be their entry and quick exit.

John gave the orders since this was his idea, and it didn't take much to persuade Ben to find the ammunition as his father owned a bakery. So, the culprit took the sacks of flour intermittently over four months. Ben's father, convinced it was one of the employees up to no good, never pinpointed the thief, little knowing it was his son.

John drew an accurate map of the site; since his father was an architect, he also inherited the talent of drawing plans, for their adventures (which were much more mischievous in their design than that of his father).

"Right, Ben, we will meet at your flat as that is where the sacks of flour are stored. We will carry one each. Do you think we have enough to cover them fully?" enquired John.

"Yep, for sure!" replied Ben enthusiastically.

"We must ensure we have one sack for each Beatle. Ian, as you are the photographer, you take the pictures. Once we are up, I will take your sack together with mine, to throw on John Lennon and Paul McCartney. Ben, you target Ringo Starr, including the drums and Gary, you aim for George Harrison. On the quick exit, Ian, you will be last so you can take as many pictures as possible," briefed John.

They had been practising sliding down metal drainpipes for many weeks, and each time became faster. The lads were now confident they could get out quickly enough not to get caught, which was crucial.

Tonight, was the night. After a quick debriefing, the lads left the flat at bang on 5 pm to ensure it was dark enough to be well hidden, dressed all in black, of course. Each of them dragged a large suitcase on wheels concealing the sacks of flour. It gave them plenty of time to get into position before the arrival of the band. They were so tense with excitement mixed in with the commotion of nerves that none of them said a word on their journey, which was a good half hour.

At last, they arrived at their destination. Leaving the suitcases hidden behind the large bins, a couple of metres away from the bottom of the ladder, John lit up a cigarette while keeping watch. More to calm him down than anything. This was one of the most elaborate schemes they had done. It took a lot of gumption and energy for them to carry one heavy sack each up to the top without being noticed. Ian almost collapsed with the weight of the bag when he reached the gantries.

"Bloomin' heck, should have spent more time with the weights!" gasped Ian, looking beetroot red and flustered, with his camera dangling around his neck, which kept getting in his way. Something he hadn't taken into consideration, but they all made it.

Much to their relief, there was a distinct lack of security guards around the back as they were more concerned about the screaming girls at the front, who'd been there since early morning. The girls were beside themselves with hysteria, which also kept the police fully occupied, trying to control the crowd rather than check behind the building where there would apparently be "no action."

The lads had a perfect view of the four rising stars, an eagle's view of its prey, one might say. Poised in their positions,

Ian was ready with his camera (top of the range), borrowed from the College for a "project" he was working on, ensuring his pictures would be top quality. John had the two sacks of flour on either side of him, and the other two lads were placed directly above their victims.

Ian was to give the signal when the Beatles were in full swing, all within range. He held his breath, trying to keep his shaking hands still. The lads, their mouths gawping, eyes fixed on him with intense concentration waiting for the signal …

Hand went down and …. PAFF!!

Their aim was spot on, as they covered the Beatles from head to toe in flour. Their band equipment was also smothered in the white powder. They scarpered down the escape route, as they had practised, sprinting away from the security guards with whistles blowing full blast. Ben tripped over a slightly raised pavement, falling head over heels onto the ground with such force, with the guards closing in on him. His heart was pounding like a steam train in full gusto as his mates rushed on ahead. As a panicked fox chased by hounds, the adrenaline in his blood spurred him to pick himself up and run as quick as a lightning bolt. The whistles and shouts were becoming more distant, so relieved that he caught up with his mates.

"Wow guys, we did it!" exclaimed John. "We bloody well did it!"

They clicked on the radio station, and already the disc jockey was inundated with hoax callers proclaiming to be the pranksters. It had reached the headlines, of which you could see them caught on film running from the scene. The lads were infuriated and wanted to announce that it was indeed them. However, they needed to stay anonymous, especially as one gang member had a girlfriend whose father happened to be a police sergeant. If the story leaked releasing their identity, they would be in serious trouble. Therefore, they made agreed to make a pact.

"We must keep this completely secret between us. Everyone, including family members, mustn't know it was us," John stipulated sternly.

The lads all nodded in agreement. Ben knew this would be difficult to keep from his girlfriend but took the vow. She was always inquisitive about his life with his mates, which he kept very close to his chest. The detective in her genes was excellent at persuading him to spill the beans but not this time, no way!

John made the call to the disc jockey announcing that it was he and his mates that were the culprits, without giving their names in keeping with anonymity.

"Yeah right, do you know how many calls we've had about this? What evidence do you have to prove it was you mate?" quizzed the DJ.

"We've got photographs from the top with a perfect view of flour falling and landing on the Beatles' heads. We can send you copies of the pictures once developed," replied John.

Ian developed these at the university, as he was in his final year of a photography degree and had complete access to the premises, which was ideal. His mates often used this facility to develop photos of their escapades, thus he was considered a valued member of the gang. The pictures were fantastic and caught the white powder's dynamics cascading out of the bags due to the ideal view. To keep the whole matter confidential, they scribbled their initials on the back of the prints to inspire the journalists' intrigue. The newspapers were soon declaring the stories and displaying the pictures on the front page, making them invisibly famous. It was rumoured to be the film crew messing about as it was the last performance in Bristol.

John was always the gang leader in their boyish pranks. They decided to concoct a story, saying that their purpose behind the flour bombing was to point to the lack of security measures. They had managed to clamber up to the gantries with four hefty bags of flour without being noticed. Indeed, they could have had evil intentions with guns and shot them. Of course, this was gibberish as they did it all for a laugh and a dare.

What seemed like a boyish prank for the others was more significant as a manic episode for John. He soon cascaded into a deep depression of vivid thoughts and nightmares concerning his father's recent death and memories of his childhood.

Chapter 2

WINSLEY, BATH 1945

As with the majority of young men in Great Britain, Daniel had also been summoned by the Government for duty to fight for his King and Country. It was incredibly heart-wrenching for him as his wife was expecting their first child in just a couple of months. It meant leaving his sweetheart, not knowing whether he would return, as the conflict became more intense. He was a reserve, with no army background and felt ill-prepared as his expertise was in the realm of architecture and property development.

He adored her, exchanging love letters over this horrific period. They had both clung to this moment when the war ended.

Dorothy, a young damsel, had decided to leave her long fair wavy hair down, wanting to look so special for her love. Standing by the front door, dressed in her favourite frock, eagerly expectant for his anticipated arrival. She had waited over three years for this occasion; often dreading the telegram of dismal news. However, she was one of the blessed ones to whom her beloved had survived the horrors of the war. She had prayed many nights for the safety and protection of her husband.

"Toot! Toot!" sounded an army vehicle which sped off into the distance. In his uniform, dark brown hair, a very handsome young man, with a beaming white smile came into focus. Dropping his suitcase to the ground, he ran towards her. Dorothy leapt into his arms as he swung her petite frame around in circles, both shrieking with exhilaration and joy.

There stood a little boy of 3 years old, hiding behind the front door feeling coy. Daniel approached him, knelt on one knee and took his cap off.

"How do you do? You must be John; your mother has been writing to me all about you," with a warm smile that reassured his son not to feel shy.

"Now, off you go and play. Your mother and I have quite a bit of catching up to do," as they both giggled like teenagers into the house.

John ran without hesitation to the back garden and climbed the small tree that was high enough for him to sit on and play.

Sadly, the excitement of the reunion was short-lived. Daniel was left shell-shocked after his war experience, shrieking out in the night with terrifying nightmares.

John would run around the house with his pretend machine gun, hiding and then making his father jump, as an over-exuberant three-year-old. Running around his feet, his father would kick him.

"Get out of the way, you annoying sod!"

He had no time for games, and for him, it was all too real. Dorothy tried to keep the lad away from his father. 'Children should be seen and never heard!' was Daniel's motto. The little lad soon learned to stay out of his way and acknowledged that he was no longer his mother's favourite boy.

Nine months later, John was introduced to his baby brother, Neil. The baby had bright red curly hair and was adored by both parents. However, his older brother saw him as another intruder and a battle between the boys was evident from the start, as he tried to get back the glimmer of attention he once had. However, it was a losing battle, so he became used to his own company.

The boys' rivalry intensified as Neil became a confident, down-to-earth young boy and John struggled with insecurities. John spent many hours in his bedroom, inventing electrical devices to prevent anyone from entering his private domain. He eventually conjured up what he thought was an ingenious contraption by connecting wire from the light fitting in the ceiling to the doorknob across the bedroom. He created a lethal weapon, via the light switch. With the light turned on, the predator waiting on tenterhooks, was ready for his victim.

At the tender age of 6, Neil dared to embark on entering his brother's bedroom. He was unable to read the sign, 'Enter at your peril!'. However, there was a clue of impending doom; a stark drawing of a boy lying flat on the ground with what appeared to be lightning dazzled on top of him. However, ignoring his big brother's warnings and not knocking (as so often was the case; hence the notice on the door) the little lad grabbed the handle.

The shock threw him across the other side of the corridor, just as his father stepped out of the bathroom. Daniel was horrified to see his little boy dishevelled in a heap at his feet. His son appeared very dazed with his red curly hair which resembled frazzled bacon! He picked him up, carefully, and carried him downstairs to his mother, who had heard the commotion whilst cooking supper.

Daniel was furious, took his belt off, and banged on John's bedroom, being careful not to touch the doorknob, "Let me in lad!" he bellowed.

The ten-year-old reluctantly disconnected the doorknob from the live source and sheepishly opened the door. Dorothy could hear the pangs of pain from her older son while reviving her infant, whose glazed eyes were beginning to focus as she held him close. John had the bizarre calibre of an eccentric and displayed concerning personality traits of schizophrenia even at such a young age.

This incident was the final straw. Both parents felt that boarding school was a viable solution for the safety of both boys. Dorothy took the initiative and applied for John to take the entrance exams. Much to his parents' relief, he achieved a scholarship and the 11+ as they couldn't afford the fees. They knew he would be better with other boys in a more structured environment. His father's belt didn't seem to deter his unruly behaviour.

John excelled at boarding school, especially with his Art and Design and earned another scholarship for college. Hidden in his studies, he managed to gain merits and awards. Girls had now entered the scene and encouraged him, and he relished their attention. Seeking a love that John longed for throughout his childhood, often felt discarded to boarding school whereas his brother stayed home. John was charming and incredibly handsome and often exchanged helping the girls with homework for new delights in the bedroom. However, it was a temporary fix and never satisfied the craving for a deeper meaning to his life.

Bristol – 1960

When John turned 18 years old, his father took him to the pub for his first "pint" as his son had now become one of the lads! Dorothy became increasingly concerned about John's strange behaviour and encouraged Daniel to come alongside him as a father. Their relationship began to develop into one of friendship as they were now both men and for once, John was just beginning to feel accepted.

"A heart attack!" shrieked his mother down the phone to John.

"Your father has had a heart attack!"

The phone was left hanging off the hook as he ran as fast as he could from the College to the car. No idea how he drove home, fumbled out of his vehicle, tripped over the threshold, and found his mother sitting in her armchair in the corner of the lounge, staring at the wall, dumbfounded and shocked. He heard sobbing from upstairs and sprinted to find his brother, aged fourteen kneeling at the end of their parents' bed, tears streaming down his cheeks. John embraced his brother and held him tight. He then noticed his father laying precariously on the bed, still and very pale. He found out that his younger brother and mother carried his father from the bathroom, where he collapsed, to the bedroom. John approached his father and checked his pulse, but nothing. He froze and wept whilst straightening his father's body on the bed and covered his face with a sheet just before the paramedics came in.

Dorothy never accepted her husband's death and eerie disturbances throughout their house, which she knew for sure was Daniel, became common. Her mental stability was beginning to affect Neil's confidence and his desire to explore intensified. He departed to Papua New Guinea to escape his family's madness and started his adventures far, far away.

Immediately after the exhilarating achievements of flour bombing the Beatles, the deep depression that eclipsed John was immense, and here he was, 23 years old in a mental asylum receiving intense electric shock treatment. The death of his father was the tipping point of his sanity. However, six months later, he came out apparently cured of paranoid schizophrenia and released into society away from psychiatric support to fend for himself.

Chapter 3

BRISTOL – 1965

"Has anyone seen Maggie?" asked Susan. "She is supposed to be on duty as Sister tonight, and I'm concerned about her, she hasn't turned up. She's always on time, often early and so unlike her?" Susan was waiting for handover, she had worked the 12-hour shift, and it had been hectic all day at the Royal Hospital for Sick Children, Bristol and frazzled.

"I saw her this morning as she was clocking off last night's shift. I told her she looked dreadful!" Rebecca was brutely honest and not always the most tactful.

"She shook her head and snapped at me, saying she just needed a good day's sleep to rejuvenate. She even skipped breakfast with us, which is odd for Maggie, she isn't one to miss a good old English Breakfast," frowned Rebecca who was also on duty tonight, as a second-year student nurse.

The rise in cases of whooping cough admissions had escalated, to the extent that almost all the wards were reaching full capacity. Children were waiting in the A&E for a bed, and Susan needed to give Maggie the update to hand over her shift. However, she was nowhere in sight. Extremely puzzled, with each minute that passed, she could feel herself panicking under the strain.

She called her manager, "Maggie hasn't turned up, and I'm worried about her, last time I saw her she was very pale and exhausted. I've tried to call, but it keeps ringing out."

Jane could hear the panic in Susan's voice. "Don't worry, I will arrange cover for her shift tonight. You go back to the nurse's quarters and see if she is at home and let me know please."

This behaviour was highly unusual for Maggie. She wasn't one to not turn up for a shift. They had relied on Maggie to work extra lately, and she had noticed she was looking skinny and seemed to be surviving on coffee.

Susan gave the handover instructions to Barbara, who was able to cover at short notice. Most of the girls lived in nurses' dormitories which meant they could focus their full attention on their careers and studies and were used to the phone ringing for another shift.

The four girls shared the same flat. Running to their dormitory, Susan noticed that Maggie's bedroom door was closed. She pensively and quietly opened the door, and there she was, sound asleep and didn't even stir. Even in the darkness, her face was pale and withdrawn. Carefully shutting the door, Susan crept into the kitchen and called Jane to let her know.

"Let her sleep, Susan. She must be exhausted! I have just been informed that she has worked 14 nights straight. When looking at her timetable not only had she worked the 12-hour shifts she has also taken on the sister of the Ward duties to the utmost and continued to work extra due to this sudden influx of whooping cough cases. Do not wake her up; let her sleep until she is ready."

Susan, Barbara and Rebecca ensured that Maggie's shifts were fully covered, taking it in turns. It was the least they could do, as she had indeed gone over and beyond helping them when they required assistance.

"Good morning, sweetheart. How are you feeling?" Rebecca spoke softly so as not to shock her. "You've got a bit more colour about you now – you looked bloody awful on Sunday Mags."

"Ah, thanks for the compliment, Becky, what's the time?"

Barbara was frying up some bacon, and the aroma was compelling – realising she was famished a bacon butty sounded perfect.

Susan went to put the kettle on to make her a cuppa.

"It's 8:30; you're just in time for breakfast."

"Breakfast!" exclaimed Maggie, horrified and somewhat confused.

"Can't be breakfast, I've got the night shift tonight." She gazed out the window to see the sun shining with the trees swaying in the light breeze and expecting to see the moon, not the sun!

Pulling up a chair, plonked herself down as Susan placed a steaming hot coffee on the table. The black liquid aroused her senses, bewildered. None of this made any sense.

"We've covered your shifts, Mags," reassured Rebecca as she placed the hot bacon butty in front of her.

"You what?! Can someone tell me what on earth is going on here?"

Rebecca could see she was looking perturbed and spoke tenderly. "We let you sleep as you were exhausted and burnt out, my lovely."

"How long was I asleep for?"

"3 days!" – the girls declared in unison.

"Oh my life, three days! What day is it?"

"Wednesday!"

Jane gave Maggie a week to fully build herself up and advised her to spend some time away from the city to convalesce.

Maggie's boyfriend, John, had recently been discharged from the hospital and she had been working so hard. It was the perfect opportunity for them to spend some time together. Just chilling and walking along the cliffs of Downderry, their 'happy place'.

It was Christmas time; the sea was at its stormiest and most exciting as the tempest of the waves always enthralled Maggie. In the middle of their 'quiet' week together, the guys and girls decided to spring a surprise on them with a barbeque.

The two classic minis drove up onto the beach.

"Beep! Beep! Beep!"

"Hey, you two love birds, surprise!"

John and Maggie were embracing and shocked to see three lads in one vehicle and the three girls in the other one. Giggling they grappled with finding their clothes desperately before their mates leapt out of their respective cars!

Maybe it was getting too quiet and what better way than mates coming over with the matches and some newspapers: sausages, beef burgers and baps loaded in the picnic basket.

John and Ian grabbed their boards. They knew it was a crazy thing to do; the waves were massive – they raced each other to the sea yelling with hysteria and excitement. The others went to find driftwood for the fire and cook the grub.

It was becoming dark, and they realised the guys hadn't come back from surfing and the waves were looking angry. Maggie and Rebecca were concerned for their boyfriends. "Where are they? They've been gone for ages?"

"Hey, there's a guy in the distance!" yelled Ben.

They frantically ran out to him; it was John! He looked shell-shocked, very pale and collapsed on the beach. The girls sprinted towards him with towels and blankets and wrapped him up. Maggie rubbed him, sobbing her heart out, holding him tight until help arrived.

"Oh my gosh! Where is Ian?" gasped Rebecca.

There was a deathly silence. She stood aghast, staring frantically out to sea with Susan holding her back from dashing into the stormy waves.

Ben sprinted to the phone box to call the coastguard.

"My mates went out to sea surfing; John has collapsed on the beach, and Ian hasn't come back!"

A search party had been called all around the area, and tragically Ian's body was never found. Their 'happy place' had become the worst nightmare any of them could imagine, and they were never to visit Downderry again.

Chapter 4

BRISTOL - 1968

A baby daughter held in the arms of her mother, Maggie looked into the eyes of this tiny infant with no hint of bonding and a gasp of pain shot across her face, only anguish and no room for love. Intense solemn emotions eclipsed this lady, the conception of a new life on the same evening of another life taken away.

She was aspiring to be an excellent children's nurse and was right at the peak of her career. However, her friend's sudden death, Ian, together with the shock of an unwanted pregnancy, led her into the depths of depression. All she could imagine was her future seemed set to be one of horror and dismay. How can a child bring so much trouble and trauma – not even an hour old?

In 1968, when you were expecting a child out of wedlock, it was considered an abhorrent shame by society. She couldn't bring herself to explain to her strict father what sin she had caused. Therefore, she decided in anguish, to marry her troubled boyfriend, John Brown. After suffering a manic episode, John received electric shock treatment for six months. Even though he had recently been discharged from the hospital, with a clean bill of health, Maggie was dubious of the recovery. Even though she loved him so much she felt unprepared for the suddenness of an immediate family and couldn't see any joy in the future.

John was exuberant with his daughter's birth and tried to perk up Maggie but to no avail; she wasn't even interested in naming the child. When he visited them, he saw that all the other babies had either blue or pink cards at the end of their little plastic cots with names written on them by their doting parents. However, after noticing that their baby had no name on her little pink card, he grabbed the label and wrote - Amber Brown. Wrapped tightly in a cream blanket, he picked up the little bundle.

"There, what a perfect name for my little girl, the daughter of an artist." He looked at her wide eyes, and for the first time in a few months, he smiled.

Maggie gave birth to Peter Brown when Amber was 18 months old. He was an adorable baby with a mass of brown hair, deep brown eyes with a placid and much calmer demeanour than his older sister, who was like a stick of dynamite causing explosions wherever she went.

The bond of love between mother and son was instant. The depression which had eclipsed Maggie began to fade away as her maternal affections centred on her son.

London 1973

All was calm in the family until one horrific morning whilst Amber was playing outside, five years old in solitude. Although she wasn't really on her own, she soon found company chatting happily to the little spider spinning his web on the dome-shaped blue climbing frame. The morning dew was a refreshment to him as he drank the lush drops of moisture which must have been enormous to the little spider, she named Charlie.

Then a man approached her, he had shaggy brown hair and wore a dark green cap. He appeared to be friendly and offered her some sweets, overwhelmed by his generosity, as he held out his hand, she walked with him. They passed the sandpit at the end of the park, which was the furthest she was allowed to go. Mummy told her that an old lady with a dog, which she could often hear barking, ate children, so she was always scared to go beyond that point.

Looking up towards the man she quietly said, "Sir, Mummy says I can't go past this point because of the dog and its dangerous."

"It's OK, you are safe with me," responded the man calmly.

The young girl was full of curiosity wondering where they were going, maybe on some fun adventure. She had promised Charlie the Spider she would return to play later.

As they passed the old lady's house with the barking dog, the man held Amber's hand, making her feel safer, so she thought, as they continued walking.

Amber instantly recognised her school and his grip tightened as they went through the doors. The little girl paused as she heard a drumming sound.

"Boom! Boom! Boom! Boom!"

She wanted to run away, but his hand became a lock.

As they entered her classroom, she saw a girl about the same age as her, at the front lying on a table, tied up with a cloth wedged in her mouth. Her eyes met Amber, the fear pulsated them both, and the image froze in her head for what would be the rest of her life. A monster hovered beside the girl, dancing uncontrollably to the drumbeat, which pounded with her petrified heart. Dressed in a black costume with the head of a weird jackal, he became frenzied with a giant knife in his hand and plunged it into the girl's heart!

She awoke suddenly with an achy tummy and a brand-new nightie, with violet flowers on it, alone in her bedroom. Slowly, with trepidation, clutching her sore belly, crept out of bed. As she tiptoed to the door, she heard footsteps and hobbled back, under the covers, shaking uncontrollably.

"How are you feeling sweetheart?" asked her daddy.

"You must have fallen off the climbing frame as I found you on the ground a bit worse for wear."

She saw bruises on her tummy, which must have happened as she fell but couldn't remember climbing.

Being told to stay in her room until she was much better and to keep her safe, her daddy locked the door. Every time she closed her eyes, the image of the girl's eyes haunted her and brought terror to her troubled soul.

Amber was left wondering – "Is this for Real?"

Was this the figment of an over-exuberant mind or a reality too chilling to recall aloud? The ruminating image in the thoughts of a disturbed child was just the start of an occurring traumatic theme that was to last throughout her childhood.

Chapter 5

SALTASH – 1973-1975

There was a commotion in the Village where they lived as a 5-year-old little girl had gone missing, and there was a frantic hunt to find her but to no avail. Amber's family left very suddenly, as there were many whispers told and secrets, hidden. Arriving in Saltash, Cornwall, far away from the drama, the family hoped to start afresh with a new life.

John was a talented graphic designer. This time he was creating a screen printing with stencils and Amber watched him in awe. She knew she had to keep very quiet when her daddy was working. He was usually in his office, which was not where children were allowed to enter, or else she was in serious trouble. However, this was quite different as he was in the playroom. Normally unpermitted to encroach on his space, he beckoned her to watch, after all this was HER playroom.

Her eyes were transfixed on his fingers as he started to cut with a scalpel on a white card some curvy shapes. Lifting it carefully and positioning the card on a screen with a wooden frame, he sealed this with white masking tape so it wouldn't move.

He pointed to a white piece of cloth on the ironing board.

"Fetch me that pillowcase Amber please."

She eagerly picked it up and gave it to her daddy.

Placing it on the table, he put the wooden frame with the cut-out picture on top of the pillowcase. He then carefully poured orange paint onto the top of the structure and with a wooden ruler scraped it from top to bottom.

Her daddy whispered to his daughter, "Shall we see what the picture is?"

He was fully absorbed in concentration as he gently lifted the wooden frame.

She imagined an orange flower or something pretty. He took the frame away from the pillowcase.

"Wow!" she wasn't expecting this …

The cut-out shapes turned into a splendid-looking horse and upon it sat a knight; however, he had no head on top of his body. He was holding a helmet under his arm, with eyes peering through it. The orange had turned paler with the white background of the material. Amber was fascinated by this design, although it was mystical rather than pretty.

Her daddy handed the finished product to her to dry, which she carefully placed on the clothes horse in her playroom.

John struggled with mental illness aspects that separated him from the world, and he often stared into the distance. His face was encumbered with sadness; Amber seemed to be the only person that would make him occasionally smile when the family gathered for their evening meal. He spent many hours in his private study tirelessly working on his next project.

Her mummy often warned Amber to never go near Daddy when he is working as he needs to concentrate, so to keep out of his way.

Maggie had no patience or time for her daughter, whom she saw as an intrusion in her life. It wasn't helped at all by Amber's behaviour, which infuriated her to the core. She tried her hardest to keep this child out of John's way by creating a playroom for the children and a lounge, for adults only, which was successful most of the time.

Amber's mischievous and somewhat adventurous personality, misunderstood as naughtiness by her fatigued mummy, was often summoned to her bedroom with no dinner.

"You can come out of your room when you say sorry!" bellowed Maggie.

"I'll never say sorry to you because I'm not!" retorted Amber crossly as she stomped to her bedroom and slammed the door in protest.

She noticed every time she was summoned to her bedroom with no dinner, the picture of the headless knight on the horse on her pillow was always facing up. During those nights, the horrors of a recurring nightmare would follow.

Instinctively she would creep into bed, dressed in her nighty and place the pillow over her head, face the wall and wait. The door creaked open and gently closed. She could feel the breath of the monster over her, and suddenly a hand on the pillow held her rigid. The agony in her tummy wretched in two, with her eyes tightly shut, keeping very still, frozen to the core. As the pain intensified, she had flashbacks of a little girl staring at her in horror, bound and shaking. The images in her mind were of a monster, dressed in black with no face with a deep groaning breath.

When she moved, often due to the pain, the pillow pressed hard causing her breathing to become shallow. The struggle ceased, and thus the monster's grip was released. When it left after a few minutes of the door closing, she was able to gasp for breath and sob herself to sleep.

Amber used to run into her mummy and daddy's bedroom frightened. Maggie became so fed up with her daughter disturbing her whilst she was trying to read her book. It was her only time of personal space as both children were in bed with John working late in the office downstairs. She concluded that the sole reason for her depression and exhaustion was her daughter whom she came to despair. The only way to resolve this intrusion of her space was to give Amber a dose of her Valium which worked a treat as she was too docile to move. The little girl never, ever went to her mummy for help again.

Amber had noticed whenever the pillow was the other side up, being plain, occurred when she was a good girl; thus, there was no horror or monster. She desperately tried to be like an angel, like her brother, who could do no wrong in the eyes of Mummy. However, to no avail, as the more she tried the angrier her mummy became. She concluded that love and acceptance were not part of Mummy's makeup towards her.

Amber knew that she couldn't make anyone love her because she was dirty and evil. As a young child, she made a vow to find a power far greater than any monster. Any love that had been experienced seemed painful and cruel, so she envisaged a journey towards hate and anger instead, as love hurt. She didn't understand what real love was and ran away into the sphere of darkness, which edged her into a world of power, intrigue and lies.

Christmas in Bath, Avon – 1974

It was Granny Winsley that opened up the world of spiritual paranormal to Amber at the tender age of 6 years old. Granny lived in a substantial family home where Uncle Neil and John grew up. The house had many rooms to explore, with a long corridor consisting of varnished floorboards upstairs with three rooms side by side and antique furniture situated in each of them. The bathroom was near the end, and Granny Winsley's bedroom was right at the end of the corridor.

Every Christmas, John took his family to see his mother, an annual event. The children would quietly play in the corner of the lounge with either two of the games placed in front of them dominoes or snakes and ladders, as the adults talked. There were often noisy disturbances of heavy furniture moving about upstairs; you could hear the double bed pushed from one end of the room to the other.

Granny Winsley banged on the ceiling with her wooden stick angrily, "Daniel, stop moving the furniture; you're making too much noise!"

The noise would immediately cease with Amber giggling at Granny being annoyed, who would then wink, "Silly man!"

The young girl was inquisitive but dared not to question because Daniel, her grandad, had died many years ago and she had never met him.

This year, the children collected the silver cutlery from the posh dressing table and began to lay the table in the dining room, in the correct order as taught by their daddy. While the adults were busy cooking and drinking in the kitchen, Amber, humming away to herself, suddenly ducked as a vase flew across from the bookshelf to the other side of the room and landed on the opposite mantelpiece. Peter cowered under the dining table in fear; however, Amber's reaction was very different, giggling uncontrollably. She embraced it as exhilarating and copied her Granny by telling 'Daniel' to move it back again. Immediately bending her knees in anticipation of impending action, it flew across the room and placed itself in its original spot. What a new exciting game she had learned.

The adults came into the dining room with the massive turkey, piggies in blankets and steaming vegetables, laughing with glazed eyes from the alcohol already consumed, from the kitchen.

"Peter, what on earth are you doing underneath the table?" shouted Maggie, pulling the shaken lad. He was too scared to say anything, and Granny Winsley leaned over to her granddaughter and whispered, "Has he been up to his tricks again?" and winked pointing upstairs.

These episodes only occurred at Granny's house, and each Christmas, it became a regular game when Amber and Peter were in the dining room on their own. She would call on 'Daniel' telling him to move specific objects and what a commotion it caused. All sorts of pottery items and even small bits of furniture, like chairs and books from the bookcase hovered in the air. Whenever an adult came into the room, the buoyant items cascaded to the floor with Amber clutching her achy tummy due to excessive laughing, with her little brother again hidden under the table.

The spirit world intriguingly was captivating to Amber, as she found an escape in another dimension away from the impending monster. When the monster crept into her bedroom, her mind would wander into this sphere of escapism. When the pain intensified, she learnt to cope with holding 'Daniel's' hand in her imagination, exploring its underworld.

Always left wondering – "Is this for Real?"

Chapter 6

KITTY

John, being an artist, was very creative and loved making things from scraps. A few days previously he made a kite, consisting of royal blue cloth for the body, and used plywood for the frame in a rectangular shape. They often went out for walks in Dartmoor and today was particularly blustery and perfect for flying a kite.

Off they went in their classic grey minivan, John and Maggie in the front two seats, with Amber and Peter who jumped into the back part which was a van and had no seats. Inside were blankets, piled on top of each other and a couple of pillows, placed for the children to sit on during the journey. These added items made it less cold and more comfortable, like a den. After all, it was the 1970s and no such thing as seat belts being compulsory, so it was deemed safe. They also had the homemade kite's company on this occasion and were excited to see it fly in the storm.

"Don't touch the kite, you two. It's not for little hands," their daddy spoke firmly, particularly glaring in Peter's direction as he was the youngest.

On the journey Peter had fallen asleep in the back of the van, so Maggie stayed with him whilst John took his daughter with his treasured kite.

They were running against the wind, and as John's excitement grew, grabbing Amber's hand and clutching his kite, he found the perfect spot to fly his contraption. He held two wooden sticks in each hand, with a mass of string tied around each one, attached to the kite's main body.

"Amber, you hold the frame still whilst I unravel the string and don't move! Don't let it go, until I say – OK?!"

He shouted extra strength as the wind was getting louder and Amber nodded in trepidation knowing how much time Daddy had spent making the kite. She wondered whether to give it a name for fun, so she called it Kitty, so she could talk to it.

The wind was quickly turning into what seemed like a storm. Amber's frame was smaller than the kite, and she clasped onto it as if her life depended on it.

"I'm giving you the biggest hug ever Kitty," as she clung onto it.

Her daddy was quite a long way off now, as he unravelled the string which blew it precariously. The wind was making it nearly impossible to hold tight onto Kitty and she was getting scared.

"It's ok Kitty I'm holding onto you with all of me!" she screamed.

"Right, let go now!"

She heard a distant cry and Daddy throwing his hands in the air with the two planks of string clasped.

Amber fell on her hands and knees as she released it. Shaking, flustered and relieved (all at the same time) that she stayed on the ground and didn't go up with it – like Mary Poppins!

The kite fled into the sky, the thick black clouds and the howling wind billowing. John grappled desperately to hold onto it, but the force of the gale was even too much for him, and Kitty disappeared into the distance. He started to chase after it whilst wailing at Amber.

"Stay there girl and don't move until I come back!"

Off he fled into the distance, leaving Amber standing there gawping at her daddy, who was running hysterically and shouting, looking like a crazy monkey!

It was nice on her own for a little bit and she found some sheep huddled under a tree trying to keep warm and approached them to have a chat. She was convinced that animals did speak because she loved watching Animal Magic on TV where they spoke to the man. Amber noticed the sky darkening, and suddenly heavy drops of water cascaded from the sky hurling and battering her small body. She began shivering uncontrollably.

Amber aware that her favourite meal was lamb chops and chips, gingerly approached the woolly sheep quietly.

"If I huddle with you, to keep me warm, I promise I will never eat lamb chops again," as tears cascaded down her blue cheeks. She was so close to them, but they ran away, bleating as cowardly sheep do.

"Fine!" she bellowed angrily at them, "I will keep eating you as you are very yummy!"

It started to get pitch black, and the fog was engulfing her, so Amber decided to try and walk to find the car as it became apparent that her daddy and Kitty were not coming back. It was like walking in the middle of a treacle storm (not that she had ever walked through treacle, but this is exactly what it could feel like). Massive heavy raindrops fell on top of her like bombs from aircraft. She imagined Muttley the dog in his plane, firing treacle pellets at her with him giggling as he did on the Wacky Races. She could see barely see her bright pink spotted welly boots and keeping her face down to protect against the gales, plodded with her legs becoming drenched and weary, she cried to God.

"God, please can you help me find my mummy and daddy as I'm really scared!"

Then, the fog started to clear a little, and she could see the outline of a minivan. She recalled her daddy's voice bellowing for her to stay put, but she bravely approached the van to find Mummy and Daddy shouting at each other inside. Amber cautiously crept to the front of the vehicle and peered through the window making Maggie gasp in fear, with her face as white as a ghost. She leapt out of the van fuming at her daughter, so it turned bright red. Amber had never seen so many colours in a face within a matter of seconds!

"We were just about to leave as your poor brother is hungry!"

Her daddy stayed in his seat, also very angry and shouting across.

"You lost my bloody kite, girl!"

Amber jumped into the back of the van, where Peter had woken up moaning that he was hungry. She grabbed a blanket and hid in it, holding back tears, of relief to be warmer but pain all at the same time. The family drove back in silence. Maggie sent her daughter to her bedroom with no dinner. As Amber took off her sodden clothes, she noticed the pillow; it was face up again. Getting changed into her nighty, she slowly crept into bed.

On the edge of her bed, lay a massive Bible Stories for Children, which Granny Winsley gave to her. It had beautiful colourful drawings, and the new desire to read the words helped her to grasp the English language. There was a man in each picture with long hair and a beard whose name was Jesus. She had never heard of Him before. Her mummy's reaction was a little weird as she laughed when Granny Winsley handed her the book, which intrigued Amber, even more, to read and look at the pictures.

The man had a child on his lap, and there were other children by his feet. He talked to them as he was sitting on the grass, a bit like their teacher at story time when the class sat on the grass when the weather was nice.

He had a kind smile on his face, and she was fascinated and adored this book. On the back, a little girl was kneeling beside the bed, hands flat together, the same as when they prayed to God at school thanking Him for the food they were about to eat. She loved the little song, "Thank you for the food we eat, thank you for the birds that sing, thank you God for everything."

She copied the little girl from the book before she went to sleep, kneeling beside her bed, with her hands together she began to whisper.

"Dear God – thank you for helping me get to Mummy and Daddy by moving the fog, the sheep didn't help me at all, but you did. I've been naughty again and made Daddy lose his kite. I am very sorry; please help me be a good girl, so the monster doesn't keep coming to hurt me. I want to be like the little girl in the book on Jesus' lap with his arms around me. Please help me to be a good girl so I can sit on his lap too. Good night God." She finished with Amen as that is how they stopped after saying grace at school. She felt a wave of warmness, which was strange but comforting.

Creeping back into her bed, put the pillow over her face and turned to the wall, just in the nick of time as the door creaked open.

Chapter 7

HIDE AND SEEK

After many doctor's appointments and hospital tests, the specialists discovered that Amber had a kink in her ureter, which explained why she was in so much pain, especially during the night. The doctor arranged for Amber to have a small operation as her kidneys were becoming damaged, and this is where she met her best friend, Natalie.

They both got on like a house on fire and became the best of friends. Natalie often had a drip by her bedside in the hospital. As they were having school lessons side by side in their beds, Natalie would accidentally knock the drip over, causing the alarms to beep as she practised her handwriting very hurriedly, which needed improving. It was not the most legible. Unlike Amber, who loved writing very neatly and in order. She would imagine her daddy smiling at her, saying how neat her writing was, like his, which was pure imagination as he never visited her whilst she was in the hospital. The girls giggled hysterically as the nurses would run around, shaking their heads.

"Oh Natalie, you are so clumsy!" exclaimed Sister Josie. "Please be careful my love, this needs to stay in your arm, not on the floor, my sweetie."

Sister Josie was so lovely and adored both girls, especially Natalie whom she saw most often and would sit by her bedside when she received her medicines holding her hand.

"Come on; everyone let's play hide and seek!" Amber's face lit up with pure delight and excitement as it was unusual to have her best friend, Natalie, come over to play. Amber was an exuberant 6-and-a-half-year-old, bursting with bubbles of energy. They were both jumping up and down, full of glee.

"Now girls, calm down a little, don't get too excited!" warned Sandra. "You need to be careful and play nicely, please."

She bent down to Amber and whispered in her ear, "Natalie is still a little frail so be gentle towards her sweetheart."

Amber saw such love in the eyes of Natalie's mummy, who was so kind.

"Yep, will do," she giggled, and they both skipped, hand in hand, to play.

Amber had a sudden inspiration for an excellent hiding place for her brother, why not the airing cupboard? Peter excitedly trusted his sister and managed to climb up to the wooden planks, and Amber smothered blankets over him.

"Shush, don't say a word and no one will find you!" she whispered.

There were spurts of ridiculous rage within Amber as his mother adored her little brother, and she resented this maliciously.

Everyone had been found, except Peter. It was a long time and no signs of Peter. When Maggie found out that he was missing, instinctively she knew that Amber knew precisely where he was.

"Where have you hidden him!?" she bellowed.

Admittedly it took quite a bit of persuading as Amber felt the power of knowing what no one else did and tottered to and fro on her feet nervously. Natalie was such a kind person and persuaded her friend to tell her mummy, so she reluctantly revealed her brother's whereabouts, but only because she and Natalie were friends. Maggie ran frantically to the airing cupboard and found her little boy unconscious. She grabbed him and realised he wasn't breathing and performed mouth-to-mouth to resuscitate the little lad and he came round.

"Get out of my sight, girl! Get to your bedroom and stay there. I don't even want to look at you. You are a mean and evil girl, and I hate you!" shouted Maggie at her daughter.

Maggie was beside herself with rage, knowing full well that Amber deliberately set to hurt her little boy. It is time for her to protect her son and ensure Amber was never alone with him. All her love and devotion will be to protect and nurture her boy from her disturbed daughter, who showed signs of mental illness which she feared that Amber inherited from her daddy.

Natalie and her mummy both left abruptly, and they didn't even say goodbye.

Amber ran to her bedroom and slammed the door. To no surprise whatsoever now, the pillow was picture up. With the imminent punishment of the monster, she crept into bed, clothed in her nightie, placed the pillow over her head and refused to cry!

The anger, hurt, rejection, and pain dwelt silently within Amber, simmering like larva underneath the ground, bubbling away. The more her little brother was loved and adored, the angrier she became, pining for a love that didn't exist for her. Deep inside her soul, she was frightened in the agony of the darkness at night. Crying to God for comfort and help, she imagined Him holding her securely in His loving arms and dancing with Him beside the river. Her imagination hypnotising her as these moments with 'God' became a solace to her and brought a light relief in the intensity of her pain.

She didn't know was the 'monster' was, but he was scary and punished her for being so naughty. As she lay there, her mind wondered who 'God' was. She made up her mind that He was kind because He helped her when she lost her daddy's kite.

Shortly after the game of hide and seek, Amber displayed some strange behaviour. Maggie noticed that her daughter was behaving nicely and becoming kind and speaking in a different voice.

"My name is Joey," she told Maggie, who went along with the game. 'Joey' was a polite girl and did what her mummy said. However, Amber remained very naughty and mischievous. Maggie realised that if she spoke to 'Joey' then her daughter would treat the task at hand much better. However, this did backfire on Amber as her mummy started to despair of the Amber 'persona' even more as she became unbearable, being so silly and backchatting. Maggie preferred the Joey 'persona'. This was the start of an inner turmoil of a split personality with voices that would argue inside the little girl's head, battling it out. Her mind became an open battleground for armies of emotions of confusion and chaos which turned to the realms of darkness.

Chapter 8

SALTASH – 1975-1977

Whooping Cough

"Hetty is in the hospital! She has reacted very badly against the whooping cough vaccine and is fitting uncontrollably," her voice was quivering, on the verge of hysterical.

"Is that you Sally?" Maggie could hear her sister-in-law panicking. "Now, slow down and take deep breaths."

"They're not sure she'll make it, and she is in intensive care," Sally gasped for air as she tried to calm herself.

Hetty was only 18 months old, usually a very bonny, bouncing baby, now looking like a lifeless doll, encased in a glass incubator. She passed the phone to Jeremy, Maggie's brother, who was always calm even in a crisis. However, Maggie froze to the core as her brother's voice was barely recognisable in dread.

"We could lose her; it's a reaction from this new whooping cough vaccine, gotta go ..."

As a children's nurse, she had heard there may be side effects of the vaccine. However, the seriousness of contracting the disease, which itself can be life-threatening, outweighed the risk of side effects.

She sat numb, thinking about her brother and wanting to rush over and see him. However, as he lived in Wakefield, it was too far to travel from Cornwall and, with her two children in tow, would cause more chaos than assistance. However, Jeremy called daily and much to their relief, Hetty recovered, and within a few months, back to being the bonny toddler.

Due to Hetty's adverse reaction, Doctor Reynolds advised Maggie that family members should not take the vaccine. Understandably, Amber and Peter were not inoculated.

Amber followed her Aunty Yvonne's dream of being a ballerina and adored dancing. She had achieved the starring role of being the head leaf in a brand-new production written by her dance teacher, Mrs Beamer. Her dress was designed and made beautifully by her mummy, made of brown flimsy fabric in the shape of a leaf. Maggie was unusually proud of her daughter, who looked elegant and wild all at the same time. Amber's face was a picture, such big green eyes full of excitement, glee and of course, mischief! The other girls were green leaves, but as the head leaf, she was brown and chuffed to bits for gaining the part.

It was a story about nature; the adventure of an autumn leaf tossed in the storm! The thrilling music captivated the young girl's soul as she danced, embracing every beat whilst pulsating across the stage. In her vivid imagination, she was surrounded by a forest full of leaves, as the other dancers twirled around her. Every move was articulated to perfection and her slight frame encompassed the part exquisitely.

Mrs Beamer, hid behind the scenes to the right of the stage during rehearsal, performing some of the moves. The dancers could look across if they needed to, for a gentle reminder.

However, Amber became the leaf with every single movement and position, with precision and perfection. She rarely looked over for support. As soon as the music played, she was lost, dancing with God in heaven and ecstatically happy.

She poured her heart and soul into this dance. This was also going to be the part she would use to audition for the Royal School of Ballet in a few months. She was encouraged wholeheartedly by her proud teacher, Mrs Beamer and Aunty Yvonne who had a few contacts at the College.

Maggie was also relieved that her daughter's ambition was the same as her sister, which began to console her. Maybe dancing could channel Amber's vibrant spirit into something more positive than mischief.

Two weeks before her performance, Amber developed a severe cough, and you would not believe the ruckus! The noise that came out of such a petite body sounded like a foghorn, warning boats of the impending doom of rocks hidden by a thick blanket of white mist. She became very sick with whooping cough that was sweeping the country viciously, like a plague. It was evident, as the day of the production approached, she would not be dancing so her friend, Emma, who had been her double, stepped into her dress on the night.

Amber was completely unaware of this with her health deteriorating very rapidly, coughing up blood and falling in and out of consciousness. Her mum never left her bedside, keeping an eye on her constantly. Maggie stepped into her role as the nurse.

She did not see this tiny, deteriorating soul as her strong rebellious daughter but as a defenceless child who needed her nursing expertise and love. Amber was too feeble to appreciate this at the time, as she coughed up more blood into a relentless supply of tissues discarded in the bin. Dr Reynolds came weekly to visit his patient and also to check up on Maggie, who looked pale due to exhaustion. After five months, Amber took a turn for the worse, as the intensive coughing badly cut her throat. Her frail skeleton shook as the vibrations rattled her frame. Dr Reynolds recommended for her to be taken to hospital urgently as he wasn't sure if she would survive the night and she required oxygen as her lungs were weak.

However, Maggie was a hardened lady, and her nursing pride declared that if Amber were to die, it would be at home, with her nearby.

Dr Reynolds reluctantly agreed and only because Maggie was a qualified Children's Nurse and arranged for the hospital equipment of drips and oxygen to be taken to her home.

Thanks to Maggie's enduring love and care, and God's intervention, the child became stronger. Each evening she would be carried to the bathroom and had a small bed beside the bath. Maggie filled the bath with boiling water to create steam; the whole room was a mist of hot vapour, the same effect as a sauna. The steam enabled the patient to breathe in the atmosphere and eased her very delicate lungs. Her brother was no longer the centre of attention, but Amber was too torpid to appreciate her mother's care.

John was pining for his wife's attention, but to no avail, then he 'caught' whooping cough, forcing Maggie to look after them both. In her desperation, she placed her daughter in their double bed, next to John. He was beckoning Maggie for some 'affection' and motioned to her to come to bed with a wry smile.

"I'm too tired!" retorted Maggie.

The familiar glare directed at Amber engulfed her mum's face. Not hearing what her mum said, Amber sat up slowly and noticed her pillow had been turned, face up. Bewildered and dazed, out of instinct, she put the pillow over her head. With her face turned to the door she watched as her mum walked away, leaving her on her own with.... the monster. The intense agony of that moment again, frozen to the core, debilitated and weak. She imagined being in God's arms as

49

her frame creaked under the pressure of the monster and heavy darkness fell upon her.

When Amber had woken up, she was at her granny and grandad's house in Bristol, in their spare room. They had picked her up after Maggie called them to take her as she no longer had any strength or inclination to continue looking after her. Amber recovered like a miracle and stayed with her grandparents for the rest of the month. No monster came, and her random chats with God increased. She adored being with her grandad, especially as he treated her so nicely and she was his princess.

Amber had been very poorly with whooping cough for a total of 9 months. Her ambition and desire to be a ballerina were dashed as she missed her audition. Amber hadn't danced for nearly a year, and her body still ached when she moved. She had forgotten all the French meanings of ballet movements as her memory had been affected by the illness.

The doorbell rang and as Maggie approached the door, she could see the outline of a skinny figure through the frosted glass.

"It's Mrs Beamer for you Amb!"

"Please, do come into the kitchen and I'll put the kettle on. Amber will be down in a little bit as I expect you'd like a little catch-up with her before she restarts her lessons for the audition," said Maggie.

As she led Mrs Beamer into the kitchen, Amber tentatively came downstairs and sat at the table opposite her ballet teacher with a somewhat sullen face.

"Is everything OK Amber? I've been concerned about you. Since you've been back dancing after your illness, your spark has disappeared, and you have decided no longer to audition for the Royal School of Ballet. You are so talented and capable so I've come specially to chat with you and your mum about how we can help you achieve this dream that you once had." Mrs Beamer's voice was calm and soft, unlike her normal matron approach at the ballet school.

"Bloody hell, Amber! What on earth are you playing at. I had no idea you didn't want to audition. This is everything me and your Aunty Yvonne wanted!" shouted her mum.

Amber just stared at them both and ran upstairs saying nothing but slamming her bedroom door with such a thud the house shook!

Maggie was so embarrassed and apologised for her daughter's stubborn behaviour explaining that since the illness her daughter's enthusiasm and even mischief had completely evaporated. Even Maggie was missing this side of her daughter and even preferred that to the sullen child, she was becoming.

"Amber is very welcome to continue classes and we shall put on hold any auditions until she is ready," said Mrs Beamer who was still hopeful that it was just a matter of time before this passion would be reignited in her top student.

Maggie was so disappointed in Amber for not even trying and cross with her stinky attitude. Her daughter had such opportunities ahead of her, and she just threw them away. She simply could not understand how awkward Amber had become since coming back from Granny and Grandad. The fragile relationship between mother and daughter has now collapsed.

Tears streamed down Amber's cheeks as she sobbed. She could hear her mum speaking to Mrs Beamer, apologising for her daughter's behaviour. Nobody understood. She wasn't stubborn; she felt deep, deep inside that she could no longer dance and was scared to step into her ballet shoes. Her dreams of dancing like Aunty Yvonne disintegrated like a dried-up brown leaf crushed in the palms of tragedy.

Chapter 9

FORDER, CORNWALL 1978-1980

Amber received the most valued present on her seventh birthday she would ever possess. Her Aunty Yvonne always bought bizarre gifts; she lived as a ballerina in Germany, and Amber quietly idolised her, she saw her Aunty once a year for Christmas.

Her mum handed her a parcel and smiled, "Happy Birthday Pickle!" she winked, "Guess who this is from?"

Written in scribbly writing on the wrapping paper, 'Love from Aunty Yvonne,' she excitedly ripped it open! A brown coloured recorder and a music book titled 'How to play the recorder book 1'.

That was it; something deep within her soul grasped this instrument. She played for hours in her bedroom, the same tunes over and over again, reciting every single note as she taught herself to read the music from the book. It became a secret message between her, and God and it felt like a connection in a spiritual way. Even though God was invisible, He was completely different from the monster. The monster made her extremely frightened and hurt her. However, God made her feel safe. After school, she would dash to her bedroom, clutching her recorder and closing her eyes would play, imagining herself dancing. Every note played was a song which produced such elation and delight. The sound echoed beautifully up to heaven, which made her feel that God was smiling. She drew from this to bring relief from the anguish experienced in the terror of the nights. Her emotions played each tune with anger, pain, hate, love, peace and comfort with each note emphasised deeply within her.

John adored classical music and would often be in the lounge on his own, playing his records. One of his favourite pieces was Vivaldi – Flute Concerto in F major which he desired his daughter to play the flute for him. He had heard that the fingering of a recorder was identical to that of a flute, and it would make a pleasant change from the persistent playing of her recorder to that of something he would enjoy far better. Therefore, it seemed to be a viable and natural progression. At her High School, the music teacher said she had the right-shaped face and would make an excellent flautist. She was captivated and inspired, having a secret crush on him. He was a tall, skinny gentleman with wild curly brown hair, similar to that of a mad professor and his charismatic character blended well with hers, she felt. Her recorder took second place as she fell in love with her flute, and this became her new soul. In her new hiding place, nothing could replace her compassion for music. So, at the age of 10, she found a new solace.

Judith, who played the clarinet at the Youth Orchestra in the woodwind section, sat next to Amber, and they became best friends.

"Would you like to stay at mine over the weekend so that we can practice together?" asked Judith.

For Amber, this would be her first time away from home at a friend's house and she felt nervous. Never, in her entire life of ten years had she slept anywhere else (other than Granny and Grandad's house during the summer holidays). Should she bring her pillow with her? What if the monster came into the room with her friend being there? Her mind became a bucket of tangled spaghetti, and before she responded, her friend agreed for her to stay.

Judith had a spare bed next to hers, where Amber would sleep. She was relieved to see the pillow on her bed was plain side up. As she investigated further, the other side was plain too, which was strange. She smiled and was so pleased that she decided to leave her pillow behind.

They practised their instruments until their fingers were aching and had such fun.

"Time for tea!" shouted Judith's mum from the kitchen.

The girls ran to the table and sat next to each other. Dad sat to their right, at the head of the table, with her mum opposite. Jack, Judith's brother, sat opposite the girls and blushed when he saw Amber and became shy. Then they all bowed their heads, Judith nudged Amber who also bowed wondering what they were doing.

"For what we are about to receive, may the Lord make us truly grateful, Amen," declared Dad with so much authority.

All the others followed with an exuberant 'Amen!' whilst Amber awkwardly followed suit. She had never prayed with her family and felt embarrassed.

The next day was a Sunday, and they went to church which was another new experience for Amber as she had never been to church before. As they entered the building, it was enormous, with massive windows made up of coloured pieces of glass that created pictures. Staring at them during the service, she could make out a man hung up on a cross.

"He was called Jesus," Judith whispered as she saw Amber's bright eyes wide open in amazement. She had never seen anything like this before.

It later transpired that it was the same Jesus as her Bible Stories book and was God's Son.

The congregation all stood up as the organ played, and the choir sang. It was beautiful, like nothing Amber had ever heard before.

"All things bring and beautiful, all creatures great and small, all things wise and wonderful, the Lord God made them all!"

Everyone sang full gusto with such passion and vigour with Amber just staring in awe and taking in the whole new atmosphere. She recognised this song as she had sung it in her school assembly and eventually joined in.

After church, she said goodbye to Judith and her family and walked down the hill towards home. Amber ran up to her mum, who was in the kitchen washing up,

"Can I go to church with Judith? She said I could go every Sunday with her if I wanted to."

Before Amber could blurt out everything about the church and choir that she saw, her mum laughed in her face.

"It's only for certain people and not you; it's only for good girls!" and carried on washing up the dishes.

Amber walked away shaking her head, as she often did, saying to herself, "Typical Mum, always putting a dampener on it."

As if her mum heard her, she shouted out, "If I ever catch you going to church, you will be grounded, do you understand me?!"

Amber slammed her bedroom door, saying to herself, again, 'Yep I know what that means for sure,' looked at her pillow, relieved to see it being plain side up, for now.

However, this did not deter her; of course, it made her more intrigued. So, every Sunday for the next few weeks, Amber secretly climbed out of her bedroom window, which was conveniently on the ground floor, to go to church.

There was also an incentive for the children to attend Sunday School. Mrs Wright, the vicar's wife, handed a little book to Amber with her name on it and smiled.

"This book is for you, Amber. Each time you come to Sunday School you will receive a sticker with a picture. When the book is full, you will receive a prize."

Desperate to get the prize she faithfully came to a few lessons. The stickers would be handed to the children, just after the first part of the main church service with the adults before Sunday school began in another room outside. Thus, she retrieved her sticker and then went straight home, without attending Sunday school, as she found it challenging to listen and became quite fidgety. Her getting into trouble with her mum was usually at the back of her mind due to the consequences afterwards. Mum hadn't caught her yet, but it was always niggling in her head.

The Sunday School teacher found out what Amber was doing and changed the procedure. The children were now to collect their stickers after Sunday School in the main church building. Disappointed she stopped attending church as it was far too risky. If she was gone too long and her mum noticed she wasn't in her bedroom, then the inevitable nightmares would follow.

At the end of the year her friend, Judith, invited her to the ceremony. All the good children got their prizes which was a whole Bible; the girls had pretty pink ones and the boys, had blue ones. Amber was saddened, knowing she wouldn't get a prize. With her head bowed down pretending to pray, she was so self-conscious, it consoled her to hide.

The vicar, in his black dress and a white collar around his neck, stood at the front. He looked in Amber's direction and motioned her to the pulpit. She started shaking, thinking she would be in trouble for not going to Sunday School and quietly went up to him, head bowed with her long hair covering her face. He was so high up on the altar part, and she sheepishly looked up.

"Well, this young lady tried her best to attend Sunday School and for her efforts, I would like to present her with a St Luke's Gospel."

He bent down and handed this to her with a warm smile. She couldn't believe it and was ecstatically happy and treasured this book and hid it in her drawer, so her mum wouldn't find it. That was the last time Amber went to church for quite some time as she got her prize.

Chapter 10

POLPERRO BARNS – 1979-1982

As the family approached their surprise destination, through the discarded rusty gate, in their classic minivan, John's face began to light up, as Amber had never seen before. He was teasing his wife by tickling her, ignoring her grumpy disposition.

"Come on woman, buck up!"

Amber and Peter were in the back of the van taking in the whole atmosphere of the beauty of the countryside. Their dad parked up right in the middle of a massive muddy puddle, John leapt out of the driving seat, not seeming to notice the mud on his trousers. 'At least his feet were protected by his wellington boots', thought Amber. They all jumped out of the vehicle, apart from Maggie, who was taking her time. In front of them were three adjoining gigantic barns with steps leading up to the front door. There was an entrance on the ground floor too. John beckoned his family to go inside, and what a sight they saw in front of them. There was just straw covering the muddy floors with broken floorboards ahead of them which were precariously hanging.

Amber thought to herself, 'This is to be our new home! I can imagine how Mary must have felt when she went into the stable to have her baby – what on earth was going on?!'

Maggie, Amber and Peter stood aghast and looked dismayed at John, wondering if he was in the middle of a mental manic episode! He tried to muster the dream in his heart, the vision of the future into them, but to no avail. Maggie burst into tears and stormed out with John chasing after her feeling angry and disappointed at his family's response.

They had purchased the property for £20,000, which was a lot of money in 1980. John thought that his family could live in the caravan whilst he did it up. The previous project at Forder was a success however that was a lot smaller, but these were three massive barns. They tried the caravan for a week, and it wasn't successful at all so before Maggie had a nervous breakdown, John decided to rent a cottage nearby whilst he renovated the barns into a palace. During this time John was working as a graphic designer and being self-employed was able to free up his time a little in-between work. Money became tight as the cottage's rent was expensive and renovating costly. However, much to John's relief, he persuaded the bank to lend him money with his charm and flare.

The day the family moved in they couldn't believe the transformation. It was beautiful, not only outside but also inside. John had converted one of the barns into a four-bedroomed property. On the ground floor were the bedrooms and up the stairs straight ahead a massive lounge with a plush beige carpet and to the left, a large kitchen diner. It was stunning, and Amber adored it. She rushed excitedly into her bedroom. It was just as she imagined with a fluffy cream carpet which made the room so cosy.

There was only one neighbour in the village, the Downing Family. Mr and Mrs Downing had three girls of similar ages to Amber and Peter: Gillian, Kathryn and Vivienne. Amber and Kathryn formed a close friendship and their adventures for the next year were to be terrific and many fond memories formed. The farmer and his wife lived at the top of the hill and there was a small village hall at the bottom which was very run down and derelict. There wasn't even a local pub or post office so very much smaller than a village, a hamlet. It was perfect for children to investigate and had plenty of space for games such as ackey 123.

Amber and Peter often walked through a field occupied by Farmer Grady's cows, which were usually docile, laying down chewing the cud as they do. This was the children's shortcut to catch their school bus from the main village, to avoid walking an extra mile along the road. On this particular sunny afternoon, the kids jumped over the stile to find themselves face to face with the cows, huddled together.

"What's up with them girls?" whispered Peter to his sister.

"Looks like we are being outstared," Amber said slowly as they carefully walked past them with the cows' gaze transfixed on the pair, heads moving as one as the kids walked.

"Their udders look particularly heavy, looks like Farmer Grady is late on milking them. Maybe we should dash for it as they're too heavy to chase us?" whispered Amber as she became more and more nervous.

Suddenly one particular cow as if she heard her, glared like an angry bull with her front two legs poised with one foot treading, ready to charge.

"Run!" yelled Peter.

Amber froze with her eyes glued onto the fuming cow and before she knew it the Friesian's two legs rose like a horse bolting on top of the petrified girl, who fell under its weight.

Peter grabbed his sister's hand, yanked her up from the ground and they ran like the clappers.

Relieved to see that due to the overfilled udders, the cow had indeed lost pace and stopped mooing frantically as they pounced over the gate.

"Bloomin' heck Amb, you just got frisked by a cow!"

When he looked over, Amber was unusually quiet as she froze to the ground, fear gripping her. Her bright green eyes were dazed, as if in a trance, and her body shaking uncontrollably.

From that day they walked the extra mile, whether the cows were in the field or not. Amber didn't want to risk it, in case that moody cow was hiding waiting for her.

Chapter 11

TREETOP RACES!

The monster didn't come as much as it used to, mainly on birthdays and Christmases. Amber suppressed any emotions of excitement during special occasions as at the end of the day when she went to her bedroom, the pillow had been turned up. Inevitably the monster sneaked in whilst she lay there, causing less physical pain as she endeavoured to 'relax' to numb these nightmares and this sordid secret remained for many years.

Amber had a remarkable escape route, that no monster or little brother could follow. It was the only place Amber could speak to God, whoever He was, in safety. She knew there was someone out there in the clouds and within the solace of the fir tree, near the heavens, He was to become her soulmate even inside the imagination of a disturbed 12-year-old.

In the field at the bottom of the Downing's house stood a spectacular splendid-looking beech tree which was ideal for climbing. Standing beside this tree was a massive fir tree, far outgrowing the beech tree by many feet. There was only one way to climb to the top of the fir which was only mastered by two adventurous girls, Amber and Kathryn. The other girls and little brother, Peter, were too timid and 'sensible' to venture to the fir tree.

The first two gigantic branches of the fir were way too high to reach from the ground. The girls would have to climb the beech tree first, its branches full of vibrant, luscious leaves. They raced each other as both were determined to be the first to endeavour the 'dare of the day'.

The trees were perfectly positioned as about three-quarters of the way up the beech, the girls were able to walk across a branch and manoeuvre onto the first thick branch of the fir. There were no leaves to dodge as this tree was completely bare of life, rotten to the core.

Then came the fun part as the only way to get to the top was to jump. Literally, jump with full gusto and grab hold of the branch above it, which was the width of a trunk. Cling to it and then heave your way onto it with heart-pounding like the clappers, then to reach the top, simple!

Amber and her mum had yet another row and with tempers at their peak, Amber charged out of the house to her place of solace where no one or monster would venture. The clouds were dark and news of a vicious storm on its way matched her mood and intensified the urgency to run to her safe place. The fir tree was now swaying aggressively as the wind picked up. The mania inside of her urged her to proceed with no thought of impending danger. Here she was, inside the stability and protection of the beech tree but not for long as she crossed to the danger of the first branch of the fir. Still furious and without any care jumped, but missed, yes, she missed the branch above her. She fell with sudden force onto her bottom to the branch she jumped off and hugged the humungous trunk petrified and stayed there for at least 5 minutes with her heart pounding in rhythm to the rocking mass of wood and storm, which was now in full swing! The drop was 60 feet and imminent death nearly encroached upon the 12-year-old. After recomposing herself, tried it again and managed to grab it, so happy and relieved. It was certainly not in her personality to let any fear inhibit her desire to accomplish the feat of the dare.

Amber spoke to God and thanked him for saving her so she could it again as she loved the adrenaline and excitement – fun fear! Why on earth should a tree defeat her?

God made this tree, 'And out of the ground the Lord God made every tree grow that is pleasant to the sight and good for food,' Genesis 2:9. Amber knew therefore that God intended for her to climb it too and was always grateful as she spoke to Him often high above the ground and near to the heavens, where she thought He may live.

However, Mr Downing heard about the near-miss as the parents had no idea that their daughters were risking their lives nearly every day and found out that the fir tree was rotten. Mr Downing's gardener chopped it down. Amber's escape – her only escape to a safe place with God came crashing down – no more safe place for a very long time for her.

Amber and Kathryn had many other adventures in the woods of Polperro Farm. These woods were situated at the bottom of the hill, in a dip on the right, just before the slope ascends to the farm where Farmer Grady and his family live. He was a short, stocky man who spoke with an extreme Cornish accent not even the locals understood him. So, when HRH Prince Charles came to visit the farm, in his white Land Rover with a convoy of security guards following, to look at the finances each year, His Royal Highness needed to bring his interpreter to translate from Queen's English to Farmer Cornish and visa-versa. They could therefore converse amicably and with no embarrassment to each party.

This small wood belonged to Farmer Grady and was his land, and as far as he was concerned his private property, and not for children to play on. Farmer Grady was quite possessive over his wood and carried a gun loaded with pellets, initially to shoot ducks for dinner but if children crossed his path, then beware!

Amber, in her pale green dress and bare feet, which were as tough as old boots (hence no need for them) and Kathryn, in her plain red T-shirt and only pair of ragged jeans and trainers, had extraordinary times climbing these 50 feet fir trees. They were planted about 40 years ago, in neat rows side by side and therefore ideal for... Tree Top Races!!!

The girls picked their fine specimens, side by side they would scale to the near top of their massive fir trees, Amber's feet hardened by the spiky trunks felt no pain as they pricked them.

The girls looked intensely at each other and yelled in unison,

"Ready, steady, go!"

They were inching their way to the top of the delicate tips which crackled and snapped as their bodies leant forward. They frantically grabbed the next treetop in front of them, letting go of the one behind broken. The girls pulsated vibrantly across their row racing each other to the end!

The sheer abandonment and unrestrained freedom of adrenaline captivated their hearts and the thrill of danger was immense, 50 feet in the heavens. Joy insatiable! Suddenly they heard distant gunshots becoming louder and louder until they saw underneath them, the fuming farmer, running around in circles. They kept still and very quiet, withholding childish giggles of hysteria rumbling inside of them, frozen fear, and enthralment mixed all together.

"I'll get you bloody girls when I catch you!" as he sped off firing another threatening shot randomly in the air.

As soon as Farmer Grady disappeared, they ran as fast as cheetahs on a hunt, to their respective homes. Amber's bedroom, being on the ground floor with the window opened for a speedy entrance, she cascaded through the window onto the bed.

She heard the old familiar voice of an angry Farmer Grady at the front door.

"Look what your bloody kids have done to my wood!"

He frogmarched Maggie outside. As they lived on the top of the hill, they could see two distinct lines of broken treetops side by side in the dip.

Amber's heart was pounding and so relieved she made it to her bedroom. Maggie flung open her daughter's bedroom door abruptly.

"See!" she exclaimed.

Amber looked up, pretending to be startled.

"What?" in a somewhat teenage sulky attitude.

"It could not have been Amber because she has been in her bedroom all afternoon as she has been grounded," declared her mum.

Which is another story!

Chapter 12

Northam – North Devon – 1982-1985

Maggie dropped her daughter off, beeped the horn of their clapped-out banger and sped off to take her son to his new school. She was in a rush to get there as a meeting with the headteacher had been arranged to ensure he would settle into unfamiliar surroundings. Maggie was running a little behind schedule and rushing around like a headless chicken in her usual style. Amber was pretty independent and capable of finding her way around and Peter needed his mother, Maggie felt.

Amber stood alone, emphasised more so, as she gazed at all the other girls being with their parents. She noticed a line of extremely expensive cars parked up by the entrance of the House.

'Maybe just as well Mum dropped me off, as 'Millie' their old banger would have looked very odd indeed,' she mused.

At the front of the House was parked an even more eloquent vehicle. The driver, dressed in top and tails, opened the majestic Rolls Royce's back door and out popped a petite Asian girl with her hair in piggy tails.

"Your Royal Highness," he bowed.

Clutching her satchel tightly to her chest, whilst the chauffeur struggled with all the luggage, suddenly a cluster of people busied around her, escorting her to the House. As this was a boarding school, it certainly wasn't quite what Amber was used to.

"This is going to be different," she muttered to herself but quite how different was an adventure to come.

The private all-girls school consisted of 4 large boarding houses; this was Belvoir. Each girl was allocated a House, whether they were boarders or day bugs, as was Amber. It was an Edwardian Mansion; the entrance was guarded by two pillars on either side of the gigantic doors, recently painted in black gloss, which were open. After the hustle-bustle of the welcome party for the Princess, she entered.

To say it was a culture shock is an utter understatement. All the girls wore the same regulated uniform, including socks and clumpy black shoes. As everyone gathered in the main hall, they were ordered perfectly, sitting on the antique floorboards cross-legged in neat rows. The atmosphere was like a library, silence with whispers of correction if one dared to move. It was austere, to the degree of Amber wondered if she was in one of her bizarre nightmares again.

Coming from a comprehensive school, the transition to this school was not easy for her. For example, whenever the teacher entered the classroom, all the girls would stand up as a sign of respect. Amber had never experienced that before. In contrast, there was a total disrespect of authority in her previous school to the extent that chairs were thrown at teachers when they entered the classroom. It was quite a raucous school, so she was thrown from one extreme to the other. To start with, and to her surprise, she did follow the crowd and simultaneously stood up as a teacher entered the classroom. However, she would never dream of being a 'posh nob' and things soon took a turn in another direction.

Hence, often rifts and tensions between herself and her tutor, Mrs Foster became frequent. Mrs Foster taught French and being an Italian lady was too rigid and strict for Amber's free spirit. Respect had to be earned for compliance to these archaic traditions imposed on her. With her mind made up, in her defiance not to comply and stand up when Mrs Foster entered the classroom, she would refuse. Of course, she took this a step further, involving all her classmates (within these six weeks of starting here she was already building up a reputation of being quite a girl.

"Right girls, when Mrs Foster comes in, do not stand up! Let's show her we are not her minions, bowing to her every command!"

Amber's face was lit up full of glee and excitement, with adrenaline rushing around her veins in a frenzy.

"I am going to dare you all not to be cowards but stay seated when the witch comes in!"

They all nodded in agreement, giggling to each other. Mrs Foster then briskly entered, "Good morning, girls!" as she banged her bag on her desk.

The room was unusually quiet. The normal chattering of pupils was non-existent, with no response, utter silence and the class remained seated. All the girls looked nervously behind them at Amber, who was sitting at the back, of course, beckoning them with her hands, enthusiastically to stay sitting.

Mrs Foster was appalled by the girls' behaviour.

"What on earth is going on here, stand up! I am not beginning the lesson until you all stand up."

Mrs Foster, with her arms, firmly crossed, somewhat bemused by what was occurring as this has never happened in all her 30 years of teaching, waited.

Gradually, as the atmosphere intensified, one by one, each girl pushed her chair back and stood up, until all were standing, with one exception, of course. Amber's face was now a bright beetroot colour, full of anger and embarrassment mixed all together in a cocktail of emotions.

Mrs Foster, with the echo of her stilettos pounding on the wooden floorboards, charged like a raging bull, to the back of the class. Peering down at the young girl in disgust, above her glasses with such a scowl her eyebrows met with each other in the middle of her forehead.

"So, it's you who is the culprit of these shenanigans, of which I am not surprised, young lady – stand up!"

"No!" yelled Amber and sped out of the classroom fuming, slamming the door behind her.

Mrs Foster chased after her, grabbed hold of her hand, frog-marched her down the corridor, plonked her on the chair outside the headmistress' office and walked away, huffing and puffing like an old dragon.

This was the first time at this school to be sat outside the headmistress' office for discipline. Still, she had only been attending for about six weeks, and it certainly was not her first experience of getting into trouble at a school.

As she sat, waiting to be called in by Miss Ball, Amber remembered Mr Taylor, the headmaster at her Primary School. Outside of his office was placed a table and chair for disobedient children. Her teacher, Mr Jasper, often told her off, usually for fidgeting, talking, and distracting the other children after finishing her work. Mr Jasper had bright red curly hair upon which a green checked berry was perched on top. He certainly fitted the picture of an eccentric artist and wacky primary school teacher. His hot temper clashed with the 6-year-old who appeared to be as vibrant as him. Therefore, he would often become intolerant towards her behaviour, setting extra work for her to complete outside of the headmaster's office. Amber would sit quietly doing her work, waiting for Mr Taylor to call her in to receive the discipline of the slipper. Apparently, Mr Jasper could even perceive when she had mischief in her eyes even before she came to start her lessons. Handing her the schoolwork set for her he scowled.

"You may as well go straight and sit outside Mr Taylor's office now. I will not put up with you today!" his face already a beetroot colour that matched his hair, mused Amber, as she sauntered down the corridor.

She often felt misunderstood but would do as she was told and sit quietly focused on her work. She had no one to distract, so she may as well do something, she thought. Mr Taylor hurriedly passed the table outside his office, like Mr Toad, she often pondered. He even had a scrunched-up face like Mr Toad too. He didn't even look at the child sitting there as he instinctively knew who it was.

"Good morning, Amber! his voice raised with stern authority.

I will call you in when I am ready."

"Yes Sir," came the sheepish reply.

It wasn't so much the slipper that Amber dreaded; it was knowing that Mr Taylor would tell Mummy, with the impending consequence of the monster which came into her bedroom that filled the youngster with terror.

The door opened briskly, which interrupted her memories and there stood an elderly lady dressed in a green and grey tartan skirt, white blouse with a lacy neckline and a v-neck pale green jumper. Perched on the end of her nose, golden framed glasses with eyes peering over the top, sternly. 'What was it with old ladies and glasses balanced on their noses, and hollow eyes in full glare' … the teenager pondered.

"What are you doing there? You are new, aren't you? And yes, I have heard much about you, Amber."

To her surprise, there was no slipper slapped at the back of her legs which was a regular outcome for her in the previous schools she attended. On the contrary, it just transpired to be a chat with Miss Ball over a cup of tea and a piece of ginger cake. The headmistress was sympathetic and kind with a gentle rebuke which is not the kind of outcome Mrs Foster had wanted. However, Mrs Foster ensured that Amber's mum was fully aware of her behaviour, and she did not go unpunished at home.

Chapter 13

A New Solace

Even though technically a day girl, Amber spent most of her time at school with the boarders until the early evening. Her parents paid the extra school fees for evening meals and homework sessions after the school day. An arrangement was put in place whereby her mum picked her up at 8 pm outside the school gates to take her to her mum's house (she never called it home as she never felt she belonged) for the night. This situation worked out very well for both Amber and Maggie as their relationship had its complexities of distance and conflict as it did from the very beginning.

However, the task of homework was very rarely achieved, so she certainly did not keep to this commitment. After dinner, she would go to Bideford town centre and stand there by the old bridge, being hypnotized by the flowing currents.

She always felt drawn by the river as it conveyed peace and tranquillity to her troubled mind and soul, which desperately needed calming. She gazed at the branches of trees that had fallen into the waters, gently meandering down the river, pondering their fate. She spoke to God, asking if she could jump and then be carried away far, far away with them.

If only she knew the words in His book that says, 'My peace I leave with you, not as the world gives, give I to you, let not your heart be troubled or afraid,' but she didn't know. Deep inside she was searching for a love that was safe, but there was only one type of love she knew, and safe, it was not!

Interrupting her sullen and contemplative thoughts, a man, unshaven and unkempt in his forties, approached her.

"Don't jump love, come and have a drink with me, and I'll give you something to live for."

His grin was slimy, his teeth looked like they had collided with each other in his mouth, all hickle dee pickle dee and his breath stank of stale cigarettes. 'Hardly the prince charming in a fairy storybook to swipe her off her feet but hey Ho!' she muttered under her breath.

However, desperate for a drink to numb any erratic feelings, Amber went with him to the local pub at the end of the town. She frequently attended this pub with different men; therefore, Sue, the landlady at the bar, knew her very well and kept a beady eye on her.

"Usual please," bounced in the fourteen-year-old with her new 'friend' of which she usually received a vodka and orange in response.

However, if an undercover policeman was present, she just received orange juice. These visitations were a regular occurrence due to the pub's reputation for serving underage drinkers. When the policeman left, the bar lady popped the vodka in there and winked with a smile.

Sue bent over the bar and whispered in Amber's ear,

"There you go my lover, get that down your neck, the copper's gone now," fixing a glare at the dirty old man drooling over the girl.

Amber remained at the bar with the man who was seated too closely, drinking (all on him, of course). Sue would be able to keep close to the teenager, even though she may be a good source of income for the pub this girl was extremely vulnerable, and she felt partly responsible for this.

Sue was serving another customer when she heard Amber giggle with a mixture of exhilaration and nervousness, an all too familiar reaction from her as the man's hands had wandered from his pint to the girl's knees. As they approached the hem of her tiny skirt, creeping up seductively to her leg, Sue yelled at the man,

"Oy! You mister, get out of my pub; that girl is only fourteen years old, you pervert!"

The hustle and bustle of the pub fell silent as the red-faced man dashed off embarrassed with his tail between his legs, literally. Amber returned to the bridge to meet another stranger for her fix. This routine was repeated until about

7:30 each evening as Amber had to hurry back to school. Frantically she ran to the toilets to change back into her school uniform, just in time to be picked up by her mum. Maggie was under no illusion that her daughter was not working hard completing her homework as the stench of alcohol was a bit of a giveaway!! She never confronted her daughter as she was relieved not to have her causing trouble at home.

Drinking became a severe problem as she needed something to numb the pain inside her soul which became excruciating. Darkness and depression engulfed Amber to the extreme of needing alcohol, in an attempt to get rid of the agony within. It did, but only for a little while.

Maggie stored some gin, hidden in the bottom cupboard in the kitchen, behind some tins. Amber clocked the bottle's whereabouts and took it upon herself to take a little bit and mix this in her orange juice for breakfast. One day, the teenager noticed, 'somebody' had drawn a line onto the bottle up to the remaining gin level. This deterrent did not prevent Amber, who carefully poured all the gin into an empty milk bottle. She then topped up the gin bottle with water precisely to the level of the drawn line. The 'milk' bottle was stored carefully hidden in her bedroom and consumed for breakfast with her orange juice with no trepidation of being caught in her tracks.

A few days later, Maggie's friend Ruth came to visit, and they both fancied some gin, so out came the bottle. Maggie was relieved to see that the alcohol had not decreased since she had drawn the line on the bottle. She poured the 'gin' into their glasses with lemon and ice.

"Cheers!" laughed Ruth as they both flung their heads back and took a massive gulp.

"Bloody hell Mags!" as Ruth spat the drink on the floor,

"Your gin has turned into water!"

"Ahhhh that flippin' girl!" shouted Mags.

Mags was not impressed but Ruth just couldn't stop chuckling all night and they hadn't had a touch of alcohol either.

Chapter 14

NATALIE

Maggie struggled with shopping bags and became more frustrated with her daughter, who wasn't helping with the heavy load, just hugging the toilet roll, the insecurities of a teenager irritating her to the core.

Still feeling the embarrassment and disappointment of the watery gin and knowing it was her daughter, Maggie exploded, entirely irrationally,

"I expect Natalie is dead by now!" she exhaled with venom.

A few weeks previously, Maggie heard the news from Natalie's mum, that she had become a Christian and that Natalie was now at peace with God. Instead of being sympathetic and understanding to her grieving friend and her newfound faith, Maggie withdrew. She was a firm believer in a spirit being, and anything resembling Christianity repulsed her. They parted company due to these differences. This news had not been disclosed to her daughter, who was very close to Natalie. John and Maggie never told Amber that her good friend had cancer of the kidneys, so therefore completely unaware of her condition.

To say this outburst and news was a shock, was an understatement, to say the least.

Something inside of Amber snapped and catapulted her to intense hatred and anger towards her so-called friend, 'God', Peter and her mum.

Running to her bedroom, she went utterly berserk and screamed,

"Why God!? Why have you killed my friend? She was such a nice girl, and it should have been me – why didn't you take me instead of her? Why God!? I will never speak to you again, and I give my soul to the devil – I will get my power from him now!"

Her deep distress echoed throughout the house as she wept until her tears were no more, with her mum laughing uncontrollably downstairs.

The next few months were to be the darkest, most troubling and most dangerous time of her life. Amber compelled other girls to form a group, with its entire focus against the Christian Union. Tracy, their leader, who infuriated her to the core with her radiant smile, became the primary target. She gathered a cluster of friends around her to form her gang, 'Devil's Lib', aiming to undermine and torment the CU. The anger, hurt, and pain buried deep within Amber, bubbling like magma under the earth's core, exploded to the surface, causing devastation all around her.

Amber became highly agitated; her behaviour was more erratic than ever. She repeatedly doodled on the cover of her exercise book frantically, 'HATE' when suddenly out of nowhere, Mrs Foster hastily approached her.

"What on earth are you doing, girl!?" she bellowed.

The fiery teacher, fuming over the defacement of her pupil's exercise book, grabbed the teenager's arm and frog-marched her to the headmistress' office – again!

Then who should casually pass her by but Tracy …

"Hi, Amber, how you doing?" smiling as her usual smiley self with no care in the world.

Embarrassed and unusually coy, astonished by her response, Amber replied a feeble, "I'm in trouble again."

They chatted for a while until the office door opened and Miss Ball popped her head around the corner.

"Time for a cuppa, Amber."

The headmistress was always so kind and it never felt like punishment as Miss Ball had a soft spot for this young lady and was so concerned about her wellbeing. She felt deep down that Amber's outlandish behaviour was a cry for help. However, as with most challenges in the 80s, these concerns were pushed under the carpet, and all vanished with a biscuit and a cuppa.

As the weeks progressed, Amber began to skip her typing lessons as she found them tiresome. She was already proficient at typewriting. Her granny owned an ancient typewriter and as a birthday gift for her seventh birthday was given a manual on learning how to type without looking at the keys. Spending many happy hours teaching herself, despite her baby finger often becoming trapped in between the massive keys, typing was now second nature to her. What was the point in having lessons when you could already type eh?!

It transpired that Tracy had free lessons and often they bumped into each other in the library. Tracy took the opportunity to spend these times just talking to Amber as she could sense that the girl was uneasy and restless. During these times Tracy was able to share her love for God and her experiences of spiritual encounters. To Amber's surprise, she felt drawn to Tracy and was beginning to enjoy her company. Her emotions became so entangled with confusion. Tracy was a friend of 'God', and Amber hated Him now. Therefore, it was urgent to arrange a cobra meeting with the gang, before Amber became brainwashed by the God squad leader.

She recalled, when she was about 11 years old, after her boyfriend, Philip dumped her, she became extremely angry and rejected. In her rage, she took her toy Snoopy outside, imagining it to be Philip and drowned it in a bucket of water and left it out to freeze.

The next day her mum was on the phone with her best friend, Ruth, as her son, Philip (who was now her ex-boyfriend), had been rushed to hospital with suspected pneumonia and was dangerously ill. Amber gasped, realising that either this was a coincidence, or she had enabled the spirit world to intervene and harm him whilst she was raging only the day before.

On another occasion, a new art teacher, Mr Jones, asked all the children to introduce themselves.

"I'm Amber Brown," declared the 11-year-old proudly, as she loved her name.

He laughed at her, "I will call you Burnt Amber as it's a dark shade of red-brown."

The rude teacher seemed to think it was hilarious. Humiliated, she turned a shade of red as the whole class giggled and she muttered under her breath,

"You will be burnt, not me," as she seethed.

The next day it was announced in assembly that Mr Jones had been killed in a car crash as it exploded, and he had burned to death. She gasped realising that her words mixed with anger were powerful and dangerous.

Amber was simmering again, coming to her senses, realising that Tracy's charm and niceness needed quashing. Something about this girl was winding her up. Amber's emotions were all over the place and she felt hypnotised, almost drawn to Tracy, which she had to fight.

"Right, I'm going to curse her to her face, and you will cover me with spells so that she will die!" her gang all nodded in agreement and giggled.

She stormed off, strengthening herself with anger and hate; Tracy was in the library in the religious section looking for a book; this was the moment. Amber hastily approached her full of fury, however, Tracy was beaming.

"I'll take that smile off her face," snarled Amber.

Attempting to open her mouth, it remained shut and wouldn't open, as if she was being gagged. Flashes of the pillow being pressed against her face and torrents of images of a girl being knifed, with dark images of a figure dressed in black, she froze. Her whole body shook uncontrollably, shocked to the core. Tracy touched her arm and looked into her eyes with such love and peace. Amber's face turned a pale blue colour and started to wretch. Tracy could see that this girl was about to throw up and grabbed the bin just in time. She put her arms around Amber and tied her hair up, so it didn't get in the way of what appeared like green phlegm from her mouth.

"Are you ok hun?" Tracy whispered.

Amber wept uncontrollably and was extremely confused. Once she had calmed down, she raised her head a little tentatively out of the bin and saw such compassion and love from this girl, who was supposed to be her enemy.

Amber ran out of the library to the dining room where her friends were waiting for her. Amber motioned with her hand for them not to say a word.

"What happened?" Kath finally said softly.

"I don't know; I really don't know," gasped Amber.

What she did know was that she saw love and a power inside of Tracy she had never witnessed before. No demons were able to get near her, and they seemed to bounce off into her instead. Dumbfounded, she was speechless, thus no trickery or witchcraft was used on Tracy ever again.

Chapter 15

Mrs Birch, the drama teacher, noticed that Amber's appetite for matters of the occult was strong. She was a believer in the spiritual world and encouraged the girls to experiment with the mystic.

The drama classes were in the basement and designed with soundproofing walls which were perfect for noisy theatrical practices.

"Right girls, I need a volunteer!" shouted Mrs Birch amongst the loud buzz of chattering students.

Rose, a member of the Christian union, put up her hand.

"Excellent Rose."

Mrs Birch placed a chair in the middle of the room, and the teenager sat down.

"Right girls. I want you all to walk around her, belittle her, and speak negatively, repeatedly to see how this would affect Rose."

Rose began to regret stepping out as this wasn't exactly what she had envisaged.

Amber leapt at the chance, and spat venom toward her, taunting her as did the other girls. Rose was becoming increasingly upset and burst into tears.

"Stop now ladies!" Mrs Birch shouted excitedly.

"How do you feel, Rose?"

Although it was pretty obvious how she was feeling, Rose was unable to reply as she could not breathe, gasping for air so her best friend, Emma, took her outside for some fresh air.

Mrs Birch seemed to have no regard for the wellbeing of the pupil at all and seemed to be getting a thrill from what appeared to be a frenzy.

"Right girls. Now I want you to look at your chair and imagine it to be a person and converse that hatred to it and then throw it."

Amber glared at her blue, plastic chair. The chair became her brother, her mum and 'God' with her anger infused, her hurt and pain of the monster, her shame, everything hurled onto that chair. She could see them sitting in it one by one, flashing across her mind vividly.

Then she grabbed it with full force and smashed it against the hard wooden floor, and it crashed into small smithereens.

The whole class turned and stared at Amber, shocked at the state of the chair.

Mrs Birch gave her the most approving smile and Amber became smitten and bashful which became the beginning of a dark spiritual crush.

Rose was eventually taken to sickbay and spent the afternoon recuperating from what is known as 'a panic attack' – the cure was breathing in and out of a paper bag.

Emma sat with her, as Rose struggled with flashing images in her mind of her school colleagues taunting her, especially Amber who was becoming very troublesome. The paper bag didn't relieve the torment but calmed down her breathing, which had become so erratic she almost passed out. Rose just couldn't get her out of her mind and when she got home (she was a day girl) confided in her mother what had happened. After hugging and many tears, her mother held her hand, and they prayed. Rose forgave her 'friend' for what she had done and asked God to speak to Amber and show her His love as it was very evident this young lady was becoming more and more disturbed daily.

Their church was arranging a video evening showing, 'The Cross and the Switchblade' adapted from a book written by David Wilkinson. It was based on a true story of a prominent gang renowned for causing violence and terror in their neighbourhood and himself, a skinny preacher man who had a heart for them to be saved.

"Why don't you invite Amber and her friends to come and watch the movie and as it will finish late, they could stay the night?"

Rose gasped, looking at her mother as if she had gone completely insane.

"Err really – she is the leader of Devil's Lib and hates me!"

"Yep, and God is bigger, Sweetheart."

Rose knew deep down that she should ask her but was full of fear and trepidation.

During the morning lessons, she recalled over and over in her mind what she was going to say to her. She plucked up the courage and walked towards her whilst Amber was on her own. She looked forlorn and less intimidating without her gang behind her.

Amber saw her approaching and was still empowered by the previous day's exhilaration of the drama lesson remembering her classmate being escorted to the sick day shaking like a leaf with her fellow friends being very silent and shocked by the whole situation.

Here she was, seemingly walking very confidently towards her. Had she forgotten the whole episode? What on earth …!

"Hi there!" Rose beamed (although that is not exactly how she felt inside at all).

"You feel better from yesterday then?" Amber responded, trying hard not to smirk.

"Much better, thank you. I'd like to invite you, Eve, Kate and Linda (aka Devil's Lib) to a movie night at my church. The film is called, 'The Cross and the Switchblade' and is a true story about a gang in America."

Her knees were clacking together, which Amber had not noticed as she was shocked and bewildered as to why on earth she would be invited to enter a 'church' of all places.

Dumbfounded, replied, "Let me have a meeting with the gang, and I'll get back to you." She walked away, her head spinning with many scenarios of the 'movie night'.

"So, what do you think girlies? We could go and cause havoc, put on our best behaviour to start with, and then show them the dark side."

They made a pact not to be influenced by any brainwashing. It was decided they would go.

Chapter 16

The weekend came very quickly, and before they knew it, here they were, in a church hall (very relieved it wasn't the actual church with crosses and statues – which always caused an unsettling reaction to their leader, Amber). The chairs were neatly in a row, and the girls were near the back. The film started, and much to their astonishment they were beginning to enjoy watching the initiation of gang membership which was gruesome and captivating. The skinny preacher man, almost compelling, as he knocked on Nicky Cruz's door. The door opened abruptly with Nicky digging his switchblade at the bottom of the preacher man's chin, threatening him with imminent death.

"Jesus loves you; Jesus loves you, Nicky!"

"Shut up man – I could slash you to pieces!"

The girls were all perched on the edge of their seats ….

"Well, Nicky – you can do that, but every single piece of my broken body will be loving you."

The door slammed in his face and the girls were silent.

The next scene was a church hall service which the gang members were invited to and sat at the back on the hardened wooden pews. The young girl was putting on a brave face, trying her best to sing. She was absolutely petrified, her knees knocking uncontrollably under her long skirt. Having notorious evil gang members in the congregation was not the average stance of parishioners, she was accustomed to. They ousted her performance, and she eventually ran out sobbing, as the mocking was just too much for her.

The skinny preacher beckoned Nicky and Israel to come forward to pick up the collection bags to pass around the people sitting quietly in the pews for an offering. Nicky swaggered up enthusiastically, shocked, and yet happy to be getting money from these unusual folk. The offering was larger than normal due to Nicky's hard stare and a demand for more money in the bag by shaking it in front of their noses.

Israel turned to Nicky and whispered, "What now? Do we run off with the money?"

Nicky looked at the skinny preacher man who was waiting for the delivery of the bags to the pulpit, his eyes facing towards the ground. There was silence. Nicky shook his head and went up to the pulpit with the congregation's eyes gripped on the pair of them.

"Thank you Nicky and Israel," smiled the skinny preacher man.

Nicky felt good and pretty cool about the situation and sat down with his gang members murmuring amongst themselves.

"Shut up man!" glared Nicky and listened to the preacher man's sermon.

After the message, Amber was bewildered as the preacher man asked whether anyone wanted to give their lives to Jesus and saw Nicky full of tears on his knees at the front praying.

Amber leapt out of her chair and shouted, "Now girls!"

They picked up the empty chairs and threw them around the room. Rose's mum gasped and grabbed hold of Amber, who was hysterical and beside herself with an emotional outburst she simply couldn't contain. They drove to Rose's home in silence. The atmosphere in the car was tense.

The girls went to Rose's bedroom, whereupon she declared,

"There are to be two of you in the spare room and the other one with me in the spare bed."

Amber hesitated. "We will need to discuss this privately." The gang walked to the spare room.

"Let's draw straws and the one with the short one has to stay the night in Rose's room," suggested Amber – the short straw was picked by Eve - they all gasped.

"No, I can't let that happen. I will take responsibility as the leader. You will have to cover me with spells," said Amber.

It was agreed and she slowly walked to Rose's bedroom who was already in her nightie and reading a book.

Amber silently got changed and got into bed.

"Are you ok?" quizzed Rose.

"Yeah, I'm fine – sorry about the church, that film freaked me out!"

Their beds were side by side with only a little gap, Rose turned out the lights and it was pitch black – as in really pitch black.

Suddenly, Rose grabbed hold of Amber's hand.

"In the name of Jesus Christ, I command the evil spirit to come out of you!" she shouted.

Instantly, Amber saw a weird demon creature hovering in the air with a massive grin on his face, directly in front of her. It had a small round face, little horns, and a tail and she also noticed another creature lying on its side on top of the picture frame on the wall beside her bed. A smaller demon than the other one who was now cackling.

"Oh no, something has gone wrong," Rose panicked.

It's ok, I can see the demons in front of me," smirked Amber.

"It's not supposed to be like this!" exclaimed Rose who couldn't see anything in the pitch blackness.

The demons were beside themselves laughing, holding their tummies and kicking their legs in sheer delight.

"You'd both better come back inside, you've freaked her out," Amber whispered to them.

Paff! As suddenly as they came out of her, she saw them fly back inside of her, laughing in her face. She felt a surge in her body and shook violently. Rose calmed down, "I think they have gone now."

"Yep, sure have," replied Amber.

The next morning Amber was extremely sick, her face a pale blue and grey and struggled to walk.

"You were supposed to cover me!" – she shouted at the girls – "That girl is crazy and did some kind of exorcism," and recalled the story to them.

She spent the rest of the weekend very poorly in bed and bewildered as to what happened and by what kind of power had this been done. She had experienced spiritual phenomena many times but had never actually seen demons come out of a person and was puzzled about how a Christian could practice spells.

On Monday, the two girls kept their distance from each other in the classroom and the episode was never mentioned again.

Amber was left wondering, "Is this for real?"

Chapter 17

The situation may never have been mentioned again, however, it was on Amber's mind constantly with the images of the smirky demons, seeing them swoop inside of her again and how she felt so sick. Her mind was engulfed with toying spirits and imaginations in her brain – it felt like strings of spaghetti being twisted around a fork and being chewed over and over without being swallowed, such was the confusion. Demons in her brain and demons in her soul, tormenting her, no peace not even when she tried to sleep – the demons would speak.

"He gets all the attention, he gets all the love, the angel of his mother, she adores him and hates you Amber!" taunted the many hideous voices. "Kill him, you deserve that love, get rid of him – your brother has caused you pain since he has been born." She saw an image of her removing her dressing gown belt – the noise of the voices in her head was getting louder, she slowly crept out of bed and went into his bedroom.

Sound asleep, 13 years old, he was breathing calmly and looked peaceful and content – "kill, kill, kill" – echoed the voices in the beat of a drum – that familiar beat of the drum and flashes of a girl, gagged and petrified the never-ending nightmare of the monster.

She calmly approached him as in a trance, clutching the dressing gown cord, slowly placed it around his neck, tied it in a slip knot, and yanked it hard! His eyes wide open gawped at her. Startled, she ran to her bedroom with the cord in her hand, heart pounding but the voices were now silent, at last.

The next moment there was her brother standing right beside her bed – the sunlight shone through the windows as it was morning time. She shot up, "Are you ok? You look like you've seen a ghost."

"Did you come into my bedroom last night and try to strangle me?" perplexed he looked intently into her eyes.

"Don't be so silly, you know sometimes nightmares can appear to be so real, can't they?"

He smiled nervously, "Yeah that's true," and off he went downstairs for breakfast.

2 Samuel 22:16-19 "The channels of the sea were visible; the foundations of the world were uncovered at the rebuke of the Lord, at the blast of His nostrils. He sent from above, He took me; He drew me out of great waters. He delivered me from my strong enemy, from those who hated me, for they were too mighty for me. They came upon me on the day of my calamity, but the Lord was my stay. He brought me forth into a large place; He delivered me because He delighted in me."

Amber's random thoughts were in calamity, rushing loudly in her brain like a steam train going like the clappers! The only way to stop it was to take lots of pills so they would stop. She tiptoed into the kitchen, hearing her mum in the room next door chatting merrily to Ruth, her lifelong friend as they studied nursing together in Bath in their late teens.

Amber gently opened the kitchen cupboard in which was stored a small Tupperware box. Inside were some tablets contained in a childproof tiny dark brown bottle marked Valium. (Maggie had been prescribed these for many years for her bouts of depression).

Hiding these in her pinafore dress pocket she crept upstairs to her bedroom and closed the door gently behind her. She could hear Maggie and Ruth giggling like schoolgirls downstairs and was relieved that they hadn't noticed her.

She remembered there was some gin left over in the milk bottle which was hidden in some towels at the back of her wardrobe. She grabbed this hastily and gulped down all the tablets with the gin. Here she was 15 years old, missing her friend Natalie so desperately, craving her companionship and someone to cry with.

Her head was beginning to feel quite numb, the voices inside subsiding. She decided to walk, more of staggering, down the long hill to the seaside at Westward Ho! It was just a15 minute walk from where she lived in Northam.

It was 9th June 1984, and the weather was unusually dull, as dark clouds hovered over intrepid stormy seas which rang riot with her emotionally battered head. Transfixed by the crashing commotion of waves, spellbound as if hypnotised Amber stepped into the cold waters. Fully dressed, wanting the sea to swallow her up, as she got deeper and deeper past her waist, she noticed the waters were becoming hotter and hotter. The waves turned a dark red, the sea was becoming like red-hot lava flowing from a volcano and the demons were now screeching so loudly, beckoning her audibly, "Die, die, die!"

Images of the little girl bound up, with Lucifer shadowing her with a large knife, suddenly turned his grotesque head and glared with dark hollow eyes at Amber walking towards him in a trance in rhythm with the drum beat of Hades. Laughing in scorn, "Come to me, Amber, it's your turn to meet me now," cackling demons surrounded her.

Completely mesmerised, she stared up into the sky and cried,

"God, help me!"

Like an instant automatic switch came the excruciating realisation that the demons were out to kill her and were not her friends. Fully immersed in the depths of the sea, arms stretched out and in a tranced state, she screamed,

"God, help me!" from somewhere unreachable in her tummy, desperate to clamber out of the sea to flee from the heat as she was approaching the pits of hell. The pull of the tide was strong trying to gulp her up and with all her might in utter desperation, she managed to reach the beach in a sodden heap.

"Tracy," she blurted out rapidly.

"I need help, please help me. I've taken an overdose and gin and tried to drown myself in the sea - I'm really scared!"

Inside the phone box, she stood drenched with people just staring at her wondering what on earth was going on. She was hysterical and beside herself with fear and panic.

"Hi Amber," Tracy said calmly.

"How about we meet outside the church tomorrow at noon and we can chat?"

"But I could die," as she scrunched up in agony in the red telephone box, the pills now taking effect.

"See you tomorrow," Tracy responded happily and she hung up.

How on earth she got home, she had no idea and still completely drenched, chucked her clothes on the floor, not caring at all, curled up in her bed. To her relief the pillow was plain side up and groaned her way to sleep. She awoke a little later than usual, but she was awake, alive in fact. Utterly dumbfounded and bewildered as to how she survived the night she ventured towards St Mary's Church to meet her 'enemy', Tracy.

There she was, in her pale grey and brown checked skirt, old-fashioned shoes and white socks halfway up her legs. She caught Amber's attention with her beaming smile, her dark brown eyes gleaming brightly; she hugged Amber with exhilaration, which was extremely foreign to her and nearly blew her off her feet.

"How you doing, Amber?" she quizzed.

"I don't know, I really don't know," was her feeble response as she lowered her head in dismay. They started walking up a small hill and as they approached an old, terraced house, Tracy knocked on the door.

"I want to introduce you to a friend of mine, Robert."

The door flew open and a vibrant, extremely handsome, dark-haired with tight curls, a tall older man, with a warm smile introduced himself.

"I'm Robert, welcome to my humble abode!" grabbed hold of Amber's hand leading her or to be more precise, dragging her to the middle lounge.

The room was full of cigarette smoke, and she could just about see a few other teenagers in the fog, drinking coffee and chatting to each other. A Chris De Burgh track was playing quietly in the background with one of the lads strumming along to it on his guitar. I'll introduce you to that lot later, as we walked past them.

"Cuppa?" asked Robert as they went through to the kitchen.

"Yes please, coffee, white but no sugar," replied Amber tentatively.

With hot mugs of coffee in their hands, passing through the thickly smoky room, and entered the front lounge. The room was void of people and smoke-free, so everyone could see each other and breathe, much to Amber's relief. She plonked herself on the old but very comfy settee with Tracy, next to her. She felt quite nervous but at home, which was the strangest of emotions and quite foreign to her, almost like a safe place.

"I understand you've come rock bottom, my love. Tracy has told me a little about you, but you tell me, what's been happening?"

Robert was filled with compassion as he listened to this young girl splutter out her soul.

She opened her heart, full of hatred and spitting venom out towards her family and God. Sharing about her spiritual experiences and how much power she thought she had until she met Tracy. She recalled the incident where her legs shook, and her mouth gagged when trying to curse her to her face. As to her astonishment, Tracy was as cool as a cucumber and just smiled as she was now. Full of love and peace which honestly infuriated her to the core.

"See, she's doing it again!" as Amber began to feel her body shaking. Whilst Robert listened to this battered and mixed-up girl after noticing some slight convulsions began to speak.

"You are full of hatred, bitterness and anger and the only people that truly love you are the young lady you are sitting next to and Jesus."

"I hate Jesus, he hasn't done anything for me!" she burst out.

Robert leaned over and motioned with his hand for her to stop spewing her hatred towards God.

"This is how much God loves you, Amber."

The atmosphere intensified as he spoke with a power and authority she had never witnessed before.

"One of Jesus' followers, who had been stealing behind His back, betrayed Him in exchange for money. To show the accusers which man was Jesus, as it was becoming dark, kissed Him on the cheek. The soldiers grabbed and arrested Him, telling many lies and ordered for Him to be crucified.

They made whips with shreds of metal, granite and glass. As they scourged His torso, the flesh would cling onto the implements and be wrenched off. Each flog pierced His body, His skin was ripped off his back, and every beating was given with full force.

He didn't make a sound.

Carrying a heavy wooden cross up the treacherously steep hill – he was so battered and weak the soldiers told another man, who was in the crowd, to carry the cross. Jesus was stripped naked and brutally thrown onto a cross with large nails being hammered into his hands and feet.

He didn't say a word.

He hung on that cross, bleeding profusely, for all your hatred, anger, bitterness, pain and in agony His final words were,

'Father, forgive them for they know not what they do.' For you, Amber."

There was silence and then sobbing and tears ran down her cheeks (she hadn't felt tears for many, many years since her vow never to cry again when she was 10 years old). These were uncontrollable tears cascading like a waterfall, the intensity of guilt, shame and immense sorrow continued for what seemed like hours. There were sodden tissues all over the lounge carpet and then a gentle voice from the other side of the room said,

"Amber, would you like to give your life to Jesus?"

Looking through bleary eyes lifting her head, Robert said very seriously, "To be honest, sweetheart, this is your last chance; because the next time you try to commit suicide, you will succeed."

She didn't understand what, "giving your life to Jesus" meant but her feeble response was,

"I suppose so," – what a choice, Jesus, whom she only heard about being an historical figure in her Children's story book or suicide. She tried that and nearly ended up in hell, which was beyond frightening. She might as well give it a go because what could she lose; it couldn't get any worse, surely.

"We are now going to pray, and I want you to repeat after me these words and picture in your mind what you are saying," Robert said quietly.

"Lord Jesus," … quietly she repeated the words.

"I believe that You are the Son of God, that You were crucified on that cross for my sins …."

With her eyes tightly shut, she saw before her a massive golden cross. It was empty, no one was hanging on the cross. She saw herself with a sack on her back full of stones and as she repeated the words, she threw the sack at the bottom of the cross.

"Forgive me for my sins, for the hatred, pain and hurt, for the rejection and anger."

She followed every single word that was being said and could feel within her being, a heavy darkness lifting off her.

"I give my life to You Jesus and I will follow You the days of my life."

Suddenly a bright light shone around the cross, she saw through the intense beam a small cross standing next to it. She picked it up, carried it on her back and walked away into the distance.

Shrieking with joy uncontrollably, she shouted "Amen!" in response.

Laughter shook her body and pulsated every part of her being. Robert prayed for her to be totally free. Wow! She ran around the room, hugging Tracy and had never experienced such joy, ever in her entire life. She was ecstatically exuberant, overjoyed and full of energy.

Robert, smiling said seriously, "Amber, I want you to know, that your walk with Jesus will not be an easy one, but you will never, ever be as low as you were when you walked through the door this afternoon."

Poem of Desperation – Based on Isaiah 53.5

God, in my frailties and vulnerabilities, where are You?
When I am pressed in and gasping for each breath, where are You?
As every weight of flesh heaves upon my tiny frame, where are You?
Frozen to the core, eclipsed by a darkness so black, no light could seep through, where are You?
Consumed with panic, numbed by an outside force, where are You?

God, when You were pierced for my transgressions.
When You were crushed for my iniquities.
When You were punished and wounded beyond any recognition.
With flesh hanging by drops of crimson red blood, bones protruding precariously.
Forsaken by all - You are there!

This was the best day of her life, Sunday 10th June 1984. Robert dropped her off at her house. Amber knocked on the door and her mum answered, she was still smiling and so happy.

"What on earth is wrong with you? What have you done?" Maggie was fuming, feeling something was not right at all with this girl.

Amber skipped around her, not caring in the slightest and ran to her bedroom.

Peter peeped through the door, "What's with you?"

"Ah, Peter something wonderful has happened to me, I prayed and become a Christian."

Everything was bubbling inside of her, and she blurted out that she was so sorry for trying to kill him last week and she loved him and wrapped her arms around him. Understandably, he freaked out. For one, she said she did try to kill him and the second one, even stranger, said she loved him. Hysterically, he cascaded down the stairs.

"She's totally flipped it, Mum!" exhaled Peter repeating what Amber had declared to him.

"Come down here and explain yourself, young lady!" came the angry shrill of her mum.

Back to the reality of home, her dad was also in the kitchen waiting for her. Turning her back to her mum in indignation, stared at her dad.

"I was suicidal and depressed yesterday, but today I gave my life to Jesus, and I am now happy."

She didn't fully understand what had happened but figured that was about right.

"How dare you!" her mother's body twisted, and she looked rather odd, thought Amber.

Maggie was more concerned that her daughter had tried to kill her son the week before rather than some religious mumbo jumbo.

However, her dad turned to her and mumbled,

"You know what, girl, you have done something far better than any of us, so congratulations!" (Referring to the religious experience not the attempted strangulation of her brother). He handed her a glass of wine, which glugged down her throat far too quickly.

Chapter 18

Monday morning, the young convert flung open the classroom door with vigour and enthusiasm looking forward to sharing her awesome experience with her closest friend, Kate. Mrs Foster was shocked to see Amber smiling, let alone leaping! With a huge beaming smile, eyes transfixed on Kate (who was also her vice president of 'Devil's Lib') and much to the shock of both of them, they screamed at each other.

As suddenly as Amber bounced through the door, she was now crying uncontrollably as soon as she had set her eyes on Kate, her partner in crime. It appeared the demons were not impressed by the conversion. Mrs Foster was forced to separate the two girls for a couple of weeks and sent them to separate lessons bemused by the whole commotion.

Rumours went around the school like wildfire – 'The leader of Devil's Lib has become a Christian!'

"Have you heard, she has become a Christian, the girl who put spells on us has converted?"

Tracy invited her to a Christian Union meeting where about ten girls usually meet at lunchtime on a Thursday.

"Yeah, sure it sounds good."

They arrived early for the meeting to have a chat beforehand to explain what a Bible study entails. One by one, the girls came, however, not just the Christian union but the majority of the girls of the school. They were intrigued to find out what on earth had happened and to hear from the horse's mouth, so to speak. The vicar who took the meeting was gobsmacked at the mass of girls trying to get into the small room.

"Right, we will have to meet in the assembly hall – we will go through and Amber, you need to explain to everyone what has happened – we all would like to know," he smiled.

About two hundred girls sat on the floor, cross-legged whispering to each other. Amber went onto the stage and looked down, very nervously she explained that she gave her life to Jesus, that she was very suicidal and desperate, and that Jesus had turned her life around, completely. Therefore, Devil's Lib is now no longer here, and I am a Christian. You could hear a gasp, murmuring even, and then one by one they started clapping. Teachers sat around the sides of the hall – some were looking happy but others seemed perplexed, especially Mrs Birch, the drama teacher.

Kate and Amber got together after a couple of weeks and agreed their friendship was no longer compatible as Kate wanted nothing to do with Amber being a 'Jesus' freak' – the group disbanded as the power of evil upon Amber had relinquished and Kate had no 'authority' to take on the role of president – so no more tribulation to the Christians, as Amber made sure of that!

Attending church was very foreign to her; it was a Church of England service, and there were men dressed as penguins at the front – or that is what it appeared. She loved the songs and bellowed her heart away, in worship to God. She heard the words of a sermon, for the first time about her newfound friend, Jesus. Then it was time for communion – Tracy explained to follow her, and she would be fine.

There were two rows of people, and she followed Tracy to the pulpit and knelt with her hands in a cup shape, just as the others were doing. A wafer was placed in her palm, and the vicar said, "The body of Christ," in a sombre and stern voice. It looked like one of those sherbet flying saucers you had at the sweet shop, rather than bread. Unfortunately, it didn't taste like it – no tinge of sherbet rather more like rubber.

Then came the challis, a vast massive silver cup with red wine filled to the brim, it looked luscious, and she couldn't remember the last time she drank alcohol.

"The blood of Christ," sternly voiced the vicar and handed her the challis.

She took a sip and ooohhh it tasted so good, so she drank some more and then proceeded to gulp down the whole lot!

The vicar grabbed the large cup and panicked looking for the bottle of wine to refill with Tracy in hysterics next to her.

This was Amber's first experience of church and much to the relief of the vicar – she had learned not to do that again, repeating silently to herself, "Just a sip, just a sip," each time she approached the altar.

Chapter 19

Usually, all the girls would celebrate graduation in a massive Marquee in one of the extensive gardens. It was a tremendous opportunity for all the girls' successes to be awarded and recognised, and the New Head Girl for the next year would be announced.

Amber received her O Level results in a brown envelope through the post. She sneaked into her bedroom on her own and slowly opened the envelope, taking a deep breath looked …

French – Grade D

Geography – Grade D

Maths – Grade C

Biology – Grade B

Music – Grade E

English – Grade D

Her dreams of going to Music College were dashed and all hopes of being a flautist playing in an Orchestra were doomed. Embarrassed, she stayed in her bedroom and cried herself to sleep.

The next morning on her way to assembly, Mrs Foster grabbed hold of her arm and pulled her aside.

"You should be completely ashamed of yourself young lady! Since you arrived at Edgehill College, you have been nothing but trouble and the standards have become a lot worse because of you.

No one has ever in the entire 100 years of this school had results as appalling as yours. Two O'levels – 2!

For this reason, you will not be presented with your certificates at the ceremony but will remain seated as the other girls receive theirs."

A few days later, everyone was excited. It was a glorious May day in 1985. The atmosphere was buzzing with excited young ladies. Amber had not mentioned anything concerning her results, only to Tracy who prayed for her. Mrs Foster led them all to be seated, and Amber ended up being in the middle of the row, chatting away to Linda excitedly giggling. The hymns were sung, this time with full gusto from Amber – she adored singing to God now, forgetting the occasion and just focusing on her newfound love for God.

Then the announcements began. Her class all stood up at the same time and were led in a row to go to the front of the platform. "Come on, Amber, get up!" beckoned Linda to her friend.

Amber stayed frozen to the spot, on her own, in the middle of the row with Mrs Foster taunting her with a wry smile as Amber's face bowed, deep red full of embarrassment and shame. Her emotions were flying all over the place, one minute so happy singing out to God and the next wanting to disappear underneath the wooden chairs.

Chapter 20

MAY 1987 – CREDITON, DEVON

Her aspirations of joining the Royal School of Music disintegrated with her failure of passing Music O'Level with a blowing Grade E. In fact, the whole class had failed, bar 3 girls who only just scraped through with Cs and their predicted grades were As, which included herself. It was an embarrassment to the school, which specialised in Music and took great pride in their previous high results. The music teacher, who was newly qualified, was abruptly dismissed. Also, to Amber's dismay her flute teacher, 'deliberately and maliciously forgot' to place her for the Grade 5 music theory exam when she was 14. She had acquired her flute exam for Grade 5 with merits with ease when she was 13 but needed to complete the theory before she could be put in for her Grade 8. Therefore, her deep desire to have completed her flute exam for Grade 8 by the time she was 15, of which she was well capable, was dashed. The truth was, however, that Amber's wayward and disruptive behaviour had prohibited her from being put forward to completing these exams as her attendance to lessons was scarce. The ambitiously talented 14-year-old had unfortunately relapsed into an emotionally and mentally disturbed teenager.

So here she was, 17 years old attending Exeter College completing a secretarial qualification instead. She consoled herself by comparing playing the flute to typing. Instead of composing music, she created words (proudly at the speed of 96 words a minute on a manual typewriter) pretending to play, 'The Flight of the Bumble Bee'. Every time she typed, she escaped into buzzing around the heavens.

In the rickety train, chugging across the meadows on the familiar track from Barnstaple to Crediton, gazing at the deep blue sky, not a cloud in sight, she was, at last, on her own. The carriage was deserted, except for a young man sitting a few seats away, who caught her eye.

Amber took a deep breath and sighed, relieved that the day was coming to an end and that she would be home soon. She had decided to visit her favourite old town of Bideford to have some time with God on the bridge, which was her place of total dreaming and escapism. However, it had transpired to be yet another spontaneous, fraught day and completely unplanned which nearly resulted in her getting into trouble, again. Trouble never seemed to be far from Amber with her unpredictable personality.

There she was looking at the swans ducking into the river to nibble at the weeds at the bottom, their legs sticking up precariously from the water.

"Hello there!" a very handsome lad interrupted her thoughts. She wasn't surprised it was so expected now. The normal spiel about, "Don't jump love, shall we have a drink?" episode, turned into her frolicking with him down by the river edge, after a few drinks. She was no longer protected by the landlady as she was 17 rather than the vulnerable 13-year-old she used to be. Teasing him, they went to Robert's house, which was always open. Robert was working, so nobody was home and within minutes they were on the double bed in the spare room, stripped naked, side by side. Amber gasped, what on earth is happening, had she completely lost her mind? He started to kiss her tenderly.

"Ah, what are you doing? Get off me!" she shrieked. "I can't do this; I don't even know your name and I'm a Christian and it's a sin," she blurted hysterically.

He lay there, starkers and speechless. Rushing out of the house, abandoning him there, she ran as fast as she could to the train station. Yet again, God rescued her from her crazy, haphazard actions. She imagined Him sitting on His throne in heaven shaking His head in disappointment, with an angel next to Him exhausted from having to get involved in helping her out again!

"Where are you going, love?"

Much to her astonishment the man sitting a few seats away was now sitting next to her. It appeared they were alone, not a single person in sight.

"I'm on my way to Exeter," he said not waiting for her to reply as she just glared at him, another intruder of her thoughts. He was quite handsome though, dark brown hair with his hazel eyes which beamed intensely at her. "Come sit on my lap."

Without thinking, she leapt on his lap. She was getting off in a few stops and he was coming off later so she could just tease him and jump off. This thought made her giggle. He started tickling her, she was so ticklish her laughing became infectious and he knew he was on to something here. She, on the other hand, was just waiting to come off the train to go home. The next stop was hers, phew!

The train halted and he shot up, "I'll help you with the door, love."

Pushing down the window of the old heavy door, he leant over outside to grasp the handle and it opened. Amber jumped off quickly before the conductor's whistle was about to blow. To her astonishment, he also came off the train and grabbed hold of her arm. Shocked, she was silent as his grip hardened. He was incredibly tall and very strong, with her petite 6-and-a-half stone frame, the young girl was putty in his hands.

It was dusk and the sun was fading beneath the horizon. He led her across the road and went through a gate into a field. He threw her to the ground, which winded her and clasped his hands tightly around her neck and squeezed. She became rigid in fear, gasping for breath and felt very dizzy. The next thing she knew the beast was on top of her. She knew that the best thing to do was to be very still, as she did with the monster in her bedroom. She clenched her eyes closed, made herself relax and let the weapon do its part. Her body became limp, as the penetrations grew stronger and stronger, turning her head to one side, his hand still tight around her neck, waited for the agony to stop.

Her heart was pounding with her eyes tightly shut, saying to God she may be coming home to see Him as she was petrified. She tried to imagine God holding out His hands. The pain ceased; the darkness was darker than dark. Remaining frozen still, moving not even a muscle, pretending to be dead, the monster eventually left. She was waiting for the door to be closed. However, after a moment she peeped, and she found herself in a field. She was on her own, crying out to God,

"I'm so sorry – I've sinned!" running hysterically home. John opened the door to see his daughter looking extremely flustered. He wasn't interested in getting involved in girl stuff and walked back to the lounge and closed the door, without saying a word to her.

Maggie and her friend Louise were just about to head off out to the pub. Amber ran into the kitchen where they were having their first glass of wine.

"Don't leave me with him tonight please Mum."

"Why on earth not!" laughing hysterically with her friend as they left the house, slamming the door behind them.

Scarpering to her bedroom, Amber blasted her record player on full volume,

"Love don't live here anymore!"

When the record had stopped, she just curled up in a tight
ball under the duvet as the pillow was picture up …

When will this struggle, battle in my soul, cease?
Will I ever be utterly free and receive inner peace?
My body has been wrenched in two by a stranger.
Masked in love but tarnished in lust, danger!

The monster shrivels it into nothingness,
As a dried, brown, fragile, fallen leaf,
Crushed into dust, in his claws with ease,
Which blows away like ashes in the breeze.

I have been discarded, rejected.
Who can love her now? He scorns
Who will love me now? She mourns
All evidence of a fighting spirit, diminished in seconds.

My soul is crushed under the weight of my sin.
Darkness consumes my heart, tormented within.
My God, please don't turn your face away from me.
Although, I deserve your wrath and scorn, than pity.

Jesus! You took my filth and pain.
When you were beaten, whipped and slain.
I cling onto You, with all my being.
Drench me in Your mercy and love.
Whilst I worship and adore You with singing!

Chapter 21

Robert's car sped through the windy roads, twisting and turning - at full pelt. A tractor was chugging away straight ahead of them in their path. Amber shut her eyes so tight and scrunched up on the front seat of the car, his foot on the accelerator on the floor! She had no idea how on earth they passed the tractor, it was taking up the whole lane. One of God's angels must have picked up the car – there would be no other explanation! She placed her heart back into her chest, from the floor of the car and laughed in hysterics of relief and fear all at the same time.

"We will get to the police station, Amber!" bellowed Robert, with both his hands in a tight grip on the steering wheel, his reddened face almost touching the windscreen.

They had five minutes to the appointment and made it, by the skin of their teeth (literally)!

Clutching hold of her hand as she reluctantly approached the station, Robert flung open the large reception door. Two police officers, both males took them both to the office. Amber was seated facing a rugged-looking Sargent, who looked like he had had too many apple pies, slouched at his desk and Robert sat in the corner. The other policeman stood up seeming to guard the door.

"So, can you tell us what happened?" They looked suspiciously at Robert, who had a reputation for being a Jesus preacher to young girls and this wasn't encouraged by the force.

After pouring out her heart, no tears, just shaking. The sin which she had committed was appalling. She had sex with a man she didn't know, a complete stranger. The shame she felt, convinced that any love God had for her had now vanished. She felt like she had jumped into the hands of the demons again, which taunted her mind.

The police officers asked Robert to leave the room, so he did. The Sergeant looked at Amber very seriously.

"Well, if you take this matter to court, you know you will have to face him. The jury may not believe you and it would be easier for you if you didn't take this any further."

He paused and frowned with his bushy eyebrows now meeting each other in the middle of his forehead.

"You do know that sex before marriage is not a sin; no matter what Robert says."

The policemen looked at each other and nodded in agreement.

"Ok," she replied feebly and had to sign a form to say it didn't happen. This was never mentioned again, and Robert withdrew from Amber with his last words to her,

"Is this for real?" "Are you for real?"

She was then left with her thoughts and heard demons cackling in her head again. Even saw images of them smirking and poking her with their forked tails, running around her in circles.

Sitting scrunched up on the bench forlorn, her coat wrapped around her body like a security blanket, with the sound of the blustery wind, she wept uncontrollably.

How do I know that You're for Real?

How do I know You are here when I
can't see You, Father God?
There came a whisper, gently in her thoughts.
Do you see the wind?
Look at the trees swaying in the breeze.
The leaves floating to the ground.
The wind is like my deep love for you, Amber.
My love blows away the dead leaves of your pain.
When your tears of anguish and grief fall down your face.
Collected in a bottle, they are held in my Heart.
Hear My heartbeat, my child, within your soul.
Take comfort in the blanket of my love.

She looked up at the trees swaying and started to rock to the rhythm and felt His arms around her, rocking her to a calm, peaceful sleep.

Chapter 22

Robert was constantly in her thoughts, she called him and left messages on his answerphone. He never replied and the rejection of the man she adored was becoming unbearable. A teenage crush maybe or an obsession because since he withdrew something inside of her yearned for his attention and love.

She heard via the grapevine that he was to be married and of all days, this happened to be on her 18th birthday. She was eagerly waiting for the invitation as surely she would be invited, after all, wasn't she still his 'little sweetheart'? Tracy and Winnie had theirs, in fact, all the girls from his gang had their invitations but not Amber. The more she dwelt upon this, the more obsessed she became. Ruminating over and over in her mind that he obviously didn't believe her, even love her and this was the proof.

Amber wanted to shut herself in her bedroom on her 18th birthday. The only part she felt she could celebrate about being 18 was that she could legally leave home. This had been a pledge she made to herself since she was 7 years old. As soon as she could get away from her family, the better.

She was informed by her mum that a meal had been arranged to spend the afternoon with her granny and grandad and they would all go to Bristol for lunch. She had loved her granny and grandad but they had become extremely distant from her and taunted her for her newfound belief in God, so visiting them was no longer the joy she had experienced as a child. No longer favoured by Grandad he judged his granddaughter harshly. Another rejection from a man she held in high esteem and adored. Little did she know that this would be the last time she would see her grandad for many years to come.

As they drove to Bristol from Crediton that morning, staring out of the window she recalled the previous Christmas in 1985. This was the only time in the year that the whole family met. Uncle Jeremy and Aunty Sally with their children Hetty, Albert and Lily from Yorkshire. Aunty Yvonne, whom Amber idolised, from Germany and then Maggie, John and their two children – Amber and Peter. Everyone was chatting away excitedly after opening all their Christmas presents. Hetty, Albert and Lily were totally spoilt which Amber and Peter always found incredibly difficult however were very grateful for what they had.

"So, Amber, your mother tells us you've found Jesus!" very drunk on the wine that was flowing since 9 am, giggled her Granny (which was more like a hiss than a laugh). Amber became a beetroot red. The whole room became silent, and all eyes became transfixed on her.

"You what, you've found religion?" taunted her Aunty Yvonne.

Everyone mocking her, like the demons in her head. Amber became angry and retorted,

"Yes, I have!"

She went on to explain how depressed she had become even to the point of attempting to commit suicide. She recalled her testimony, walking into the sea wanting to drown and how Jesus had completely changed her life as she found inner peace and joy. As she remembered her encounter with Jesus her face beamed and the whole room became unusually quiet, even the smaller children were looking up from playing with their new toys. Granny transfixed a glare at her through her large framed glasses, the entire time. After Amber's 'sermon', Granny withdrew to the kitchen to prepare the turkey dinner.

Nervous laughter echoed from all members of the family, teasing the forlorn teenager for the rest of the day. She prayed it would be the last Christmas she would have to spend with them. Her Aunty Yvonne just shook her head disappointedly at Amber, whispering in her sister's ear. The frowns and mockery from her mum were to be expected but never from her Aunty. The silent admiration of her ballerina Aunty was crushed in an instant.

Amber had been reading a Christian book which she had left on her pillow in her bedroom, looking forward to taking some comfort from the words, crept upstairs to get away from the noise. However, she was surprised to see that her book had been replaced with a book on the occult. She heard a floorboard creak as someone followed her, turning around. There was her Granny.

"We do not allow religious books in his house young lady, and it has been replaced with something real and not fairy stories!"

She laughed, hissing as she walked down the stairs back to her family.

Retrieving her small pocket-sized Bible hidden in the bottom of her suitcase, Amber lay under the covers with her small torch secretly reading, as she did when she was at home. For words of help, she always turned to the book of Psalms. She whispered so that only Father God could hear her.

"Please Father God, speak to my heart as I'm hurting again, you heard them laugh, you heard them scorn, Amen."

The words popped up out of the Bible, like a picture pop-up book she used to read as a child.

"To You, O Lord, I lift up my soul.
O my God, in You I trust.
Do not let me be ashamed or my
hope in You be disappointed.
Do not let my enemies triumph over me.
Indeed, none of those who wait for You will be ashamed.
Those who turn away from what is right
and deal treacherously without
cause will be ashamed.
Let me know Your ways, O Lord.
Teach me Your paths."
Psalm 25:1-4

She lay on her bed, resting her eyes, the images in her mind becoming vivid. She was in the secret garden, a beautiful array of brightly coloured flowers dancing in the breeze. She followed the footpath, through the high hedges, dancing. There was the swing, and she saw herself leaping, in a pretty summer dress towards the plank of wood hanging precariously by two ropes tightly fastened to the Beech tree. She knew Father God was in the garden and the safety of His presence enveloped her. The Psalmist's words hummed in her ears, as she entered the warmth and security of His embrace.

Lord, as I approach your beautiful
holiness, melt all the dross.
You crush all that says, "no" as I bow before the cross.
All that You died for, all that You cried
for, Your tears of compassion.
Draw me nearer, nearer to your awesome
presence, my Father God.

As I crumble under Your love, as I bow before Your face.
All that is deep within surrenders,
where there is no disgrace.
Because You have released me from
harm, by the power of the sword.
I enter into the warmth and security of You, my Lord.

Back to the present, they arrived in Bristol, Granny and Grandad were waiting for them at the restaurant. They had reserved a table and were in the waiting area.

"It's the birthday girl!"

Grandad was waiting for his granddaughter to greet him and they exchanged a polite hug as she was too big for proper hugs now and everything was a lot more formal since that final Christmas, two years ago.

"Hello, Grandpa!"

She even had to call him Grandpa now as he had become suddenly rich due to his brother's business doing extremely well. His shares in the company enabled him to gain a small fortune. It was like the money had changed him overnight, thus pomp and ceremony were introduced. Amber obliged as she could be polite when it meant she could profit from a lovely meal. However, she would always see him as Grandad.

Chapter 23

The relationship between Amber and Peter was a lot less turbulent than during their childhood. Amber's newfound faith meant that she was learning not to pine attention from her parents. They were quietly chilling upstairs and chatting amicably about God. Peter hadn't dared to talk to his sister about this previously, as their mum was adamant to keep them apart. Mainly due to her concerns about Amber's mental health being 'brainwashed' and she certainly didn't want this to affect her son.

They managed somehow to sneak a little time together as their mum went to the shops. However, they didn't hear her come back.

Amber was in full flow of telling her testimony and asked her brother if he would like to give his life to Jesus. He had observed the sudden change in his sister, from being so hateful towards him to voicing love. He was extremely cautious as his mum had said it was just a phase and each day wondering when she was going to change back to her nasty self. This phase had now lasted 2 years. After hearing her story for the first time, he realised that there were tears down his face and he so desperately wanted to experience the deep love Amber was speaking about. He was just about to say yes when …

Maggie had been listening by the door and furious that her daughter was up to no good again, flung open the door.

"What do you think you are up to, young lady? I heard you putting strange ideas into his head."

Her face was getting redder and redder, glaring at her son, "So, what is it then Peter, you have a choice – you choose – Jesus or me?"

Peter started shaking, there was no way he would manage without his mum, she was his everything and the bond between them was very strong. Her bright blue eyes were now transfixed on him.

Stuttering nervously, "I choose you, Mum."

Laughing hysterically, stared at him – "Then I possess your soul, you are mine forever!"

Turning to Amber, "You, get out of my sight, get out of this house and take your religion with you!"

Running to her bedroom Amber slammed the door. Desperately, throwing some clothes in a bag precariously, ran out of the house with her mum shouting,

"I never want to see you again, get out!"

Peter was silent, looking withdrawn and extremely unhappy.

This wasn't quite how she had envisaged leaving home. She was glad to be out of the house for good, but where would she go? She stayed with her friend's family for a couple of nights to gather her thoughts.

There was a knock on the door and there stood John. Her friend hesitantly let him in and shouted upstairs.

"Amber, someone is here for you?"

Intrigued, the young teenager crept downstairs to see her dad in the corridor and frowned.

"What are you doing here?" he mumbled.

"Your mum has told me you left the house in a temper with some clothes and asked for you to come back."

"She told me to leave and never come back. She's the crazy one, there is no way I want to live with that woman again!"

John couldn't disagree with his daughter.

"Fair enough, all the best girl," and off he went.

Her friend's dad overheard the conversation.

"Sounds like she didn't chuck you out, you just wanted to leave. I'm going to suggest you go now as we can't have you here any longer."

"Are you for real Amber!?" he bellowed.

"Liars do not go to heaven and I don't want you near my daughter again!"

She picked up her belongings and couldn't say goodbye to her friend who had been sent to the living room.

Out on the street again. 'Where to go now? What to do? Father God, where are You right now, she pondered?' She found a park bench as it was becoming dark, wrapped herself in her blanket and shivered herself to sleep. A drip from the tree above dropped on her face mingled with her tears streaming down her face.

Chapter 24

After qualifying at college Amber had managed to get herself a job as a legal secretary in Exeter which was going well to start with but then after a couple of months with her head being all over the place, she made a huge error (whilst typing about 50 letters – very fast and incredibly proud that she had accomplished so many letters for a partner of the company (as his secretary was on holiday). The letters were all dictated onto a tape and then played back and typed diligently on an electronic typewriter. Amber handed the tray to Mr Drake who was very impressed with the number of letters she had done. Pen in his hand, head bowed down ready to sign – he suddenly drew a line straight across one, back in the tray, then the same with another letter, back in the tray.

"What on earth is this?" he scowled extremely angry and becoming quite red.

"It is Messrs and not Mrs for a company, did they not teach you anything at college, are you stupid?!"

She had never even heard of the word Messrs and apparently this is what he said for the company name and every single letter had been rejected. She went from being so proud to just wanting the floor to gobble her up.

"You will need to do these all again tomorrow!" he bellowed.

We are talking retyping the whole lot as these were the days before computers and typex (correcting fluid) was certainly not accepted by a firm of solicitors. There were to be no errors, they had to be perfect.

The next morning, she was asked by Mr Board, who was the senior partner, to go to his office for a private meeting. He was such a kind and gentle man and enjoyed Amber's vibrant personality and was not looking forward to this at all.

"I'm so sorry my girl, but we believe you are not suitable to be a secretary for this company and therefore give you two weeks' notice to find another job. Your mind seems to be all over the place and your lack of concentration is very noticeable. This role needs to have a more focused worker."

He encouraged her to try something outside of an office environment which would be a little more stimulating to suit her temperament. He was sad to see her go as she did replace the mundane atmosphere of law with a vibrancy he and his fellow Solicitors certainly lacked. He was forced into a corner by a red-faced Mr Drake who kept repeating that she was stupid. However, Mr Board was sure there were other reasons for this but was told to find someone a little more stable and reliable and just 'get rid'.

Mr Board wanted to give Amber two weeks of breathing space to find more suitable work or maybe she would get her head together and show his grumpy fellow partners of the company that she had it in her and prove them wrong. He also thought that the word, 'Messrs' was outdated as we were now in the 1980s not the 1880s and if they weren't teaching this in college maybe they were the ones in error, not a young 18-year-old with potential.

Amber thanked Mr Board for the opportunity of working for the company and shared a little with him about her precarious situation at home and that hopefully, she will settle soon. Mr Board was the kind of gentleman that you could confide in, reminded her a little bit of her grandad when she was a girl.

Mr Board smiled, "You're a good girl and I'll miss you."

He gave her a gentle hug and a wink as she left the room.

Chapter 25

So here she was, the prospect of no job, in an unfamiliar place as they had just moved to Crediton with nowhere to live. There was no one to call except for Robert who hadn't spoken to her since the episode with the police a few months ago. She had to pluck up the courage as God hadn't said anything to her, so she was really on her own.

In the telephone box, she dialled the number and he answered, "Robert speaking."

"Robert, it's me, Amber! My mum has chucked me out and has possessed Peter's soul, David has called me a liar and thrown me out and I have nowhere to go. Please can you help me?" she blurted out at top speed hysterically.

Bursting into tears uncontrollably and shaking, there was silence on the phone.

"Not much I can do here in Cheltenham, Amber. I am married now and can't just drop everything to see to your disasters every five minutes. I will give my friend a call. Her name is Helen and I'll see if she can help you. Give me the phone box number and stay there." He hung up.

Not that she had anywhere else to go, so she stayed in the phone box as it was pelting down with rain but left the door slightly open, so she wasn't suffocated by the weeing smell in the corner of the box.

It seemed like ages and wondered if the lady had said no and with her mind racing pondering what else to do, the phone rings.

"Right Amber, I've told Helen where you are, and she will pick you up and have a chat with you to see if she can help. That's all for now," and he hung up.

There was a queue forming for the phone box, so she sat on the wall, soaked but relieved that someone was able to help her. Her life was like snakes and ladders, she seems to make a little progress and suddenly lands on a snake and has to go all the way back to the bottom. Here she was rock bottom, feeling very abandoned and rejected by everyone.

She was grateful to Robert for bothering with her and knew that this would perhaps be the last time he would as he voiced his frustration with her and now he was married, she was no longer the centre of his attention.

Maybe this was the opportunity for her to start again, to start afresh. To be honest with this lady and maybe even give her life back to Jesus, just in case He had abandoned her too – which due to His lack of voice felt very apparent.

She hadn't been the best disciple of Jesus and maybe He was angry with her, like the monster used to be when she was living at home.

She has now left everything, all her possessions were at home, including the pillow which her dad had made her when she was little and was the subject of so many nightmares and pain. Maybe now, she would not feel that agony and maybe she could really say sorry to God and start again. Often in her thoughts, she wondered whether she had sinned too many times since being a Christian. Did Jesus die on the cross and forgive those sins as well, after He had delivered her from past sins or had she blown it? Had she gone too far and that's why she was always in trouble? Had God also turned His face away? Maybe her mum was right and she was the one with the issue and the lies were all in her head.

The beep of a little horn brought her back to reality, "Is that you, Amber!?" shouted a voice from an old classic grey mini.

Helen had assumed it was, as this young girl was looking very bedraggled, lonesome with her head in her hands, sitting on the wall by a telephone box.

Raising her head out of her hands, and peering up she saw a rather large lady, in her fifties, in the smallest car. Amber ran over and opened the door to see a rather shaggy small dog lying on the floor of the passenger seat.

"Hello, yes I'm Amber," she hesitated to wonder if the shaggy dog was friendly or whether it was an ankle biter!

"Get in girl you're letting the rain in the car! Don't worry, Jasper has already eaten so he won't eat you!" Helen giggled.

Amber laughed nervously and crept in trying not to disturb Jasper. The shaggy dog was half asleep looked up and went back to sleep again, much to her relief. She wasn't used to dogs, her family always had cats, which weren't seen as pets on the farm but as mice catchers. Her view was animals outside and humans inside.

They arrived at a beautiful cottage, with Ivy around the frame of the front door and the driveway reminded her of Granny Winsley's gravelled lane. Shoes were placed inside the porch and the smell of lavender was so homely – Amber began to relax. They approached the kitchen and an elderly man was by the kettle.

"I'm Pa!" he went over and gave the girl a massive bear hug. He was a skinny man, with fair brown hair and the warmest of smiles.

"I expect you'd like a nice hot drink, tea or coffee young lady?"

"Coffee please, white and no sugar."

"On to it my lover!" in the broadest of Devonshire accents.

Helen and Amber went into the conservatory – wow! It was the cosiest and most spectacular room Amber had been in. Inside grew a huge vine, with grapes hanging down, two wicker armchairs and a small glass table in the middle with quaint white crochet placemats.

"Please sit down and let's have a chat."

Helen appeared to be quite strict and seemed to have that headmistress way about her.

Amber knew that this was the chance to start over again, to be completely honest and she poured out her heart.

Helen listened to this troubled teenager, explaining about the monster, the nightmares, the sin she committed with the strange man and how painful it was like the monster. She poured out her heart that she didn't know who the monster was, that she was always such an evil girl, that she was a witch but gave her life to Jesus who helped her. However, she still got into a lot of trouble and therefore Jesus was cross with her, and she needed to be punished. She didn't know if the demons in her head were real which she saw since a little girl. The reoccurring flashbacks of the girl who was stabbed in front of her by a monster in black. Every single thing she could possibly think of that had happened in her 17 years of life she blurted out, so she could start over again. Helen just listened and Amber was beginning to feel a little better hoping that she understood. They had stopped for a few breaks with lunch and an evening meal and then she finally stopped.

"I'd like to commit my life back to Jesus and start afresh," said Amber.

Helen just stared at her and what came next shocked Amber to the core.

"Ok, I believe you have a huge problem Amber, with lying. Everything that you've said to me today has been a pack of lies. There is no way you don't know who the monster is. There is no way that your nightmares weren't real as they are too detailed. You are a compulsive liar and until you tell me the truth, you are out of this door and on the street. I have a friend who has said she will take you in, she has a spare room and is a Christian. However, if you are not prepared to tell me the truth then I do not want her to have you stay with her. I suggest you go upstairs young lady and pray and be prepared to tell me the truth."

Helen pointed upstairs and Pa gently nodded. She pleaded that she told the truth, but Helen declared that she knew from the Holy Spirit that Amber was lying.

She knelt beside the bed on her own and prayed.

"Father God, I'm in trouble again – you heard what I said, I told the truth, but she said that you said I have lied so I am very confused. Is this for real? I'm going to be homeless. I thought you were going to help me. I am really, really sorry God, but I am going to go downstairs and tell a pack of lies so I can have somewhere to live. I wanted to start again and have a fresh start by telling the truth. It looks as if lying is the only way forward. Please forgive me, God. I am now going to lie."

There was silence. She looked at the pillow, it was plain so at least the monster won't come tonight, she thought. Then remembered she had left the pillow behind and therefore the night-time terrors were to be no more.

Pa had made a fresh coffee and sat with them at the table, which put Amber a little more at ease.

"Are you ready?" quizzed Helen.

The teenager took a deep breath, "Yes" she replied.

Then she spewed out the lies, the stories that she thought were not real, saying they were real.

Chapter 26

"Welcome to our home," Claire spoke softly as her foster daughter, Esther, was sleeping upstairs.

They entered the kitchen and drank hot chocolate. She was in her fifties and when she smiled, this exposed a protruding front tooth (she was a Nanny McPhee lookalike thought Amber). She came across as quite strict but with a gentle demeanour.

They crept upstairs. Claire quietly opened the bedroom door.

"This is your room, sorry it's a bit small," she whispered.

To Amber, it was perfect and the first thing she did was look at the pillow. It was a plain one, no picture, the relief of a peaceful night. The first night in her life when things have gone terribly wrong, she lied and yet would not be punished. To her amazement she couldn't sleep, it felt inconceivable not to experience agony after what she felt was like an unforgivable sin, she knowingly lied to live here. She found herself scratching her arm with her long nails until she bled which gave her a small sense of relief.

"My God, I am so sorry, wash me clean. You know my heart, I wanted to tell the truth. I know liars don't go to heaven, please forgive me, please …"

Tears of remorse trickled down her face as she sobbed herself to sleep with her arms throbbing. A new alternative to punishment, but would this suffice for God, she wondered?

She had not yet had the revelation that Father God's Son, Jesus Christ, whose scarred body, brought about by the brutality of whips made by men, had taken this punishment on Himself. However, this mindset of self-abuse to ease the pain of guilt was to remain with her for many years to come.

Claire invited Amber to attend a local church in Exeter and everyone seemed very friendly, all very polite. Although she did wonder what was hidden under those plastic smiles and how many approved of her 'ungodly' background. Claire felt it would assist Amber if she moved in with Linda, Carrie and Davina. These ladies were in their 30s and would be a good example for her to follow and learn the appropriate behaviour of a Christian. They were all single, waiting patiently for the man of their dreams and here was Amber, approaching 19 years old with three boyfriends all at once!

She was struggling, however, to keep them separate but managed to make up different stories to each of them to achieve this. Mark was Mondays and Tuesdays; Geoff was Thursdays and Fridays and she saw Simon for weekends.

Wednesdays were a little breather and her quiet time with Father God. It was workable but to say the girls were not happy with her for being so dishonest was an understatement. Amber couldn't decide which one she liked the best. They all had their different characters and she adored them all.

Mark was tall, dark and handsome with big softy eyes and reminded her of a teddy bear. He was always very nervous and a bit insecure, but he was lovely to look at.

Geoff was of small stature, with ginger curly hair, bright blue eyes and a lot of fun. He had charisma and when Amber was manic, he was perfect to do very silly things with.

Then there was Simon, who was fair-headed, glasses and looked like your typical 'Christian' guy with old-fashioned trousers and a bit of a geek. However, he had money and for weekends took her out for nice meals and was very knowledgeable about the Bible which she found fascinating.

She needed them all and they all wanted to go out with her, so she did. This was much to the dissatisfaction of her housemates who were not quiet about their disapproval explaining that it was ungodly behaviour. Amber knew deep down that they were correct but didn't want to admit it and she was having so much fun.

"You're all old and fuddy-duddy," the teenager giggled as they shook their heads in dismay.

Then, on one Wednesday evening, (which was her day off with the girls at home and her quiet time) the doorbell rang, and Linda answered it.

"Amber – ummmm, it's for you!"

As the youngster approached the door, Linda stared at her crossly, as she hurried back into the kitchen.

To Amber's shock and amazement, all three of them were standing at the door. One had flowers, the other chocolates and the other just himself.

"Hello, this is a nice surprise?" she shrieked.

They all looked at each other and then at Amber who impulsively introduced them to each other and brought them into the lounge in deathly silence. She left them to it and rushed back into the kitchen where the other three girls stood there with mouths wide open gawping at her.

She could hear quite a commotion with the guys, then the front door slammed shut leaving an eerie echo. The girls all turned their backs on Amber who was sitting at the kitchen table. She sheepishly entered the lounge and found Mark sitting on his own, forlorn, with a small box in his hand. His head was bowed and looked devastated.

He didn't look up, just stared at the box and gently opened it to reveal a diamond ring!

She gasped and thought to herself, what on earth was going on? Was this for real?

"I was going to ask you to marry me, but you've broken my heart, Amber."

She stood speechless, as he walked past her, placing the box in his trouser pocket, with his shoulders slouched and left.

She took herself to her bedroom and sat on the bed. The penknife was beside her lamp, her new form of monster. The guilt consumed her, "I'm so sorry God, I've messed up again!" Gripping the penknife, scrapping her arm over and over, blood dripped onto her bed sheets as the pain intensified, fully deserved. Her head pounding with the images of the three guys standing at the door, the three girls glaring at her and God, turning His back on her. She sobbed herself to sleep, again.

She awoke to a silent household, as she crept downstairs there was no one at home. She looked at the clock in the kitchen and gasped. She had overslept and it was Sunday morning and church was due to commence in 15 minutes.

Sprinting upstairs, she grabbed what she wore the previous day, put on extra deodorant and a splash of perfume instead of her usual shower.

She peered at her watch and had made brilliant timing. The church building, which is a school during the week, was unusually quiet. In fact, it was ghostly quiet, the street seemed people-less and there were no cars in the car park.

She could see through the windows that the building was empty. Had the clocks changed? No, as it was July. She had heard sermons recently about the imminent return of Jesus Christ. She panicked and immediately her heart began racing, convinced that Jesus must have returned and forgotten about her. It became obvious to this young, troubled soul, with her thoughts escalating, that her behaviour the previous day with the three lads had been seen by Jesus and this was the consequence.

She walked very slowly back home, again the house was void of any life whatsoever. Sitting on the bottom of the step, devastated, she repented – really, really repented. She shouted at the top of her voice,

"Oh God, I am so sorry for all the sins I have committed, all the lies I have told, all the horrible things I have done. Please forgive me God, please and pick me up and take me with you? Please, God!"

Closing her eyes, with her arms up at the bottom of the stairs, yearning for Jesus to pick her up. Maybe He can't because I am in the house, she thought, so she went outside.

As everyone had gone to heaven, there wasn't anyone to see her, so she didn't care. She threw her arms up and stretched up, jumping, "Pick me up, Jesus, I'm here and I'm really sorry …"

With her eyes tightly closed hoping to see Jesus in a vision – nothing.

Tears streaming down her face, she opened her eyes and saw the three girls walking towards her.

"Oh no, Jesus has forgotten you too!"

The girls looked dumbfounded at her, "What on earth are you on about, Amber?"

It came to light that the school building was being used for something else and the church met in another building. As Amber hadn't attended church the previous Sunday and the girls forgot to mention it, hence the empty building wasn't due to the return of Jesus.

Thus, extremely relieved that Jesus hadn't come back to pick up His flock, she tried her best for a few days, just in case she was caught off guard again. Soon forgetting the wake-up call, it wasn't long before she got into trouble again.

Chapter 27

Her housemates were always concerned about Amber's behaviour and advised her to get some help. Linda was always straight with her.

"Have you spoken to the minister, you need counselling or deliverance?"

She agreed, her emotions were always so up and down, one minute manic and doing very bizarre but extremely fun things and the next minute, in her bedroom hiding, cutting her arms and feeling suicidal.

Linda agreed to accompany her as a meeting had been arranged for Amber to see the minister and the girl was fearful as she had never received counselling before.

It was in a very pleasant area of Exeter and the houses were large. The car park was full, but they managed to find a space. The minister and his wife, Susan, welcomed them both and to their bewilderment, there were about 8 men in the lounge. She recognised a few of them from the church but not all of them. Not saying anything, they were introduced to everyone and there was a chair placed in the centre of the living room.

Amber was asked to sit down in this chair, facing the minister who spoke.

"I understand from Linda that you are having a difficult time and we are here to help you. Everyone here is in the Ministry and would like to have more practice in the field of deliverance. Please, tell us about your experiences with the occult and witchcraft."

Amber sat there and was taken aback a bit. She didn't know what to expect but this felt quite bizarre.

She hesitated but just kept her eyes on the minister, forgetting the audience around her and spoke about her childhood meetings with her dead grandad, items moving from one end of the room to the other, the effects of the voodoo snoopy doll on her boyfriend, at the age of 9. She never said a word about the 'monster'. It seemed she was provoking a realm of delight around the room. After she finished sharing her stories, silence.

"Thank you for sharing, Amber. I understand it must have been difficult for you."

Although she wasn't convinced that he did understand, as some kind of wry smile came upon his face.

"We are now going to pray for you and each of us will take it in turns. Don't be distressed and close your eyes."

The minister spoke softly with that wry smile becoming wider and gave her the creeps.

Linda nodded at her, in reassurance.

Here she was sitting in the middle of the sitting room, with about 8 men circled around her.

The minister came up and laid his hand upon her head and shouted, "In the name of Jesus Christ, I renounced these demons and tell you to get out of her – what is your name demon?"

He raised his voice more, Amber blurted out a word, 'hate', as she wasn't liking what was happening to her and her body began to shake in fear.

Then another person came up and put his hands on her head, "In the name of Jesus, you evil spirit of hate, get out of her!" and everyone joined in with shouts of, "the blood of Jesus and get out."

Inside she felt weird. It was similar to when Robert had prayed for her. Her body went into spasms, and she screamed. Suddenly the men held onto her, and one man lay on top of her, shouting in her ear. She felt pain inside like when the monster hurt her and screamed even more. The audience became frenzied and so excited. Amber was petrified, the more she screamed the more pain she felt. There were flashbacks of a man dressed in black with a large knife in his hands, soaked in blood, taunting her inside her head. She saw images of a young girl gagged with a bloody handkerchief and bound by a rope and fear enveloped her. She knew the best thing to do here was pretend to be dead and become still, as she had done in the past with the monster. To be frozen and then she was sick all over the carpet.

When it had all finished, everyone left mumbling in ecstatic excitement together,

"Wow, did you see that, and what happened there!?"

Linda gently took Amber's hand, who was feeling very numb, as if hypnotised. The minister's wife had a bucket of hot water and soap, cleaning up the sick from the carpet and said reassuringly,

"Don't worry about the carpet my lover, the demons have come out now and you are free."

In the car, nothing was said. When they arrived home Linda whispered,

"Are you OK, Amby?"

Amber looked dazed and couldn't reply so Linda led her upstairs to her bedroom and sat next to her on the bed.

Linda noticed there were many bruises all over her young friend's arms and legs. She took the nightie from under Amber's pillow and between them slowly and carefully managed to get her ready for bed, her tummy was black and blue.

They were both silent as Linda held Amber in her arms and rocked her to sleep, as they both sobbed.

The girls never went back to that church and the event was never mentioned again, as if it never happened. Amber contemplated yet again,

"Was this for real?"

Chapter 28

Mark graciously forgave Amber, and they began dating again, ensuring that the other two guys were out of the picture. He enjoyed her company and due to her being so volatile wanted to be the man to protect and look after her. He could see she had recently become very withdrawn though and she became reluctant to step outside her home, unless he was there by his side, which he liked, but puzzled as very much out of character for Amber.

He tried to get to the bottom of what was wrong, but she was adamant that she just needed to start afresh at another church and didn't want to say. He respected this and took the opportunity to invite her to his church.

All was relatively calm until the recent arrival of some Americans, to evangelise Great Britain. He was told by these American folk, that to be with your girlfriend alone could put a man at risk of falling into sin and for that reason, courting was done with a chaperone. Mark, therefore, introduced his girlfriend to his sister, Lorraine, as their chaperone, just in case he was tempted to seduce her as he did find her very attractive.

Lorraine was a bubbly character, quite the opposite of her brother and the girls got on like a house on fire and they immediately became good friends. This helped Amber come out of this agonising shell and they chatted more easily than she did with Mark.

Mark and Amber were now engaged to be married. The American preacher persuaded many young people to come out of their home churches of 'Mum and Dad' to venture out to his newly formed 'church'. It was based in Dartmoor, which had evil connotations for Amber and unpleasant memories where witches would gather for rituals and ceremonies in her nightmares. She thought it was very strange that a church would deliberately put itself in the centre of witchcraft. Maybe they didn't know or maybe this was in her head, so they wouldn't know, would they?

Mark wanted a blessing, so he informed the American preacher (Pastor Chad) about their engagement and was keen for him to marry them. However, Amber was very suspicious of the American, mainly because she was sceptical about anyone calling themselves a 'minister of religion'.

The meeting commenced and after singing a few hymns it was time for the sermon. Pastor Chad starts to prophesy to the young people in the congregation. He points to Mark.

"I have a word for you, Mark."

Captivated, he hung onto every single word and this preacher proceeded to say,

"You have to get rid of your heart's desire and follow me."

Pastor Chad gazes across to Amber, who was looking at him suspiciously, (Mark had his eyes closed and head bowed).

"Thus saith the Lord!"

With the identical wry smile of a 'minister' peered at her and nodded as he went for his next victim, she felt.

Pastor Chad then proceeded to share a vision he was seeing in a loud declaring voice of authority.

"A dark cloud is moving from Dartmoor to Doncaster and a move of the Holy Spirit is on its way there. You are to sell everything you have, as it mentions in the Book of Acts and to give your profits to me. I will then distribute the wealth evenly amongst the group."

He finished the vision with, "Thus saith the Lord!"

There were four families, with young children, shrieking with delight and as far as Amber and Lorraine could tell were hypnotised with frenzy. Mark was also full of exhilaration. Pastor Chad went on to give details of buying a large bus and they would then travel together to Doncaster and evangelise.

Then he stretched out his arms, swaying them like palm trees being blown in the wind, towards the people who seemed again hypnotised by the preacher. Everyone jumped off their seats, flying across the room with chairs scattered everywhere. People were falling all over the place, and lying on the floor laughing like hysterical hyenas, except for Lorraine and Amber who stood and just stared at them all.

The preacher proceeded to yell at the girls.

"You are evil, and I renounce you devil to get out of them! Get out!" he bellowed.

Looking at each other, they were quite happy to depart, being careful not to tread on the congregation who were now sprawled across the wooden floor.

"What on earth was that about? I'm not comfortable about this at all," frowned Lorraine.

This was her first visit and could now understand why Amber was concerned. She had wondered whether Amber was paranoid because of her previous experience of 'church' in a minister's lounge, which she courageously shared with her.

After the meeting, Mark approached Amber.

"You heard what the Lord said, you are my heart's desire, and I will therefore have to break off our engagement. I am moving to Doncaster after selling all I have."

"You idiot!" shouted Amber.

"Can't you see what he is up to? I heard what that man said, but just because he adds on, 'Thus saith the Lord,' doesn't make it true."

"Sorry," Mark shook his head devastated that he had to break it off.

Lorraine was furious with her brother and didn't mix her words on the way home either.

It later transpired that four families did sell their properties and handed all their money to Pastor Chad and his wife to share amongst the group. They purchased a large blue rickety bus, and all went (including Mark) to Doncaster. After a few days, the preacher and his family went back to America to visit friends with the promise of coming back to continue with evangelism. The money, of course, was put into his personal bank account and he and his wife never came back. These young families had lost everything, in a place that was not their home.

It was alarming to see how one man could influence and brainwash these young people. They trusted the words of a man believing that it was God leading them. He used scriptures and persuasive words for these people to give up everything. Their lives were ruined by a false preacher.

Amber pondered in her heart, 'I expect they will never allow this kind of event to occur again. I sincerely hope that God restored everything that this 'locust' had eaten. He is a just God and sees the hearts of people.'

She was glad that her heart was guarded, and she wasn't persuaded by this pretentious man and woman. She was shocked to see those innocent souls become gullible and it is a lesson to be so careful not to be deceived.

The enemy comes like a light, he is the perfect deceiver. Eve was tempted by the fruit looking so nice with the lie from the serpent that God was being mean, but the truth is that Father God protects His people and loves us. It can appear to look good and seem like a really good idea but it so isn't.

"The love of money is the root of all evil," You say.
Consumed by greed and corruption, "pay," they say.
The kind-hearted, gentle folk, trusted,
sold everything and gave.
Lost all their treasures and became enslaved.

These ministers of religion acted in
disguise, in Your Name.
Innocent souls, pulled by enticing words, in Your Name.
"Why do evil men prosper and the
righteous stumble in poverty?" I say.
"Do not be concerned, My child.
All men will give account on Judgement Day."

Chapter 29

On holiday in Ibiza, the men stared and would never leave the girls alone which annoyed them both. They were sunbathing, topless, to fit in with the crowd. Amber was conscious of feeling naked and this was the first time she had exposed her body to the public arena. To Amber's shock, her housemate gasped as she took off her top.

"Wow, you've got quite big breasts, haven't you? You hide them under your big baggy jumpers – you need to show off your figure more, girl!" declared Davina.

This was the start of an agonising obsession and life-threatening condition for Amber.

Slightly taken aback she had never seen herself as a big girl, only being 5 foot 2 inches tall. When she looked in the mirror, Davina was right. They seemed heavy and ugly as did the rest of her, she felt. This is when the deception took place unnoticed, especially by herself.

"Either they get bigger with men drooping all over them or they go," she muttered to herself. So they disappeared, as she ate nothing for weeks, just drank black coffee but to her mind, they seemed to be getting larger.

Amber became inspired by a film she had recently watched about how a young girl became very skinny and her boobs disappeared.

"Perfect," thought Amber, "Big boobs, time to be dissolved!"

At 5ft 2 inches and 7 stone, Amber considered this a weight too heavy and wanted to reach 6 stone. A month later she succeeded but felt even heavier. It became more difficult to lose weight, thus she established a routine of making herself sick every morning and most evenings, by sticking her finger down her throat to reach 5 and a half stone. When she succeeded, it still felt too heavy and endeavoured to conquer 5 stone.

After some research, she learnt that laxatives helped to reduce weight. She tottered off to the chemist and bought 200. It said on the bottle to take 2 in the evening, but it seemed to have little effect so putting 10 small tablets in 5 bundles on the bed, she gulped them down with a large glass of water and hey presto! they worked. She accomplished losing 3lbs overnight and so carried on taking them as well as being sick.

The agony was unbelievable as she curled up on her bed with a hot water bottle in absolute excruciating pain, swearing that she would never take them again. However, she'd weigh herself the next day and the loss was noticeable. So, it became a habit, 75 in the morning and 50 in the evening.

Despite the pain and inconvenience at 2:00 am having to get up and rush to the loo, she carried on. The urge to lose more weight was too strong and her welfare didn't matter. She didn't care about the pain and was determined to be 4 stone no matter what it cost.

She became a cold, irritable and hard person which she knew was something God did not like. In a trap which she couldn't get out of, the only thing constantly on her mind was to be 4 stone. The fixation on calories and weight was on the verge of being obsessive.

Depression never had such a meaning as now, consumed by an everlasting black hole.

Paranoia began to clasp its grip on Amber as she became convinced that people around her disliked her grotesque body. She constantly felt dirty, untidy and so ugly and her vibrant personality had vapourised quite a while ago. As she peered in the mirror and stared at her morbid frame, she could understand why so many comments were taunting her. Even her closest friends in the house poked fun saying that she possessed the appearance of an old woman, apart from Linda.

As Amber put the kettle on for yet another black coffee, she hadn't noticed that Linda was sitting at the table in the kitchen with a mug of coffee and a piece of toast. Linda had been waiting for the opportune time to chat to her and as the house was quiet, the other girls had gone out, now was the moment.

"Amber," said Linda, which made the girl nearly spill the boiling water on her hand as she jumped a mile.

"Bloomin heck!" exclaimed Amber. "You made me jump out of my skin!"

Which to be honest was now a regular occurrence, as she was becoming jumpier and more irritable lately.

"We need to talk, my love." Linda spoke gently and motioned to the chair opposite her at the kitchen table.

Amber's heart dropped and beat ten to a dozen all at the same time. She didn't want another meeting with the previous minister and his weirdo friends. It was since that episode that she had become so paranoid and apprehensive about any man.

She must have read her thoughts as Linda responded, "Don't worry, no more ministers delivering demons from you, sweetheart."

Amber was surprised she even mentioned this as they hadn't talked about it since. One of those, 'Is this for real?' episodes, which on this occasion seems to have actually taken place. However, before she could dwell on this any further Linda leant over and held her hand.

"You should see your doctor, sweetheart, as you are just not your normal self, and I am concerned about you."

Amber was not impressed.

"There's nothing wrong with me, I'm fine and I don't need any help from anyone!"

Burst into tears and ran upstairs to her bedroom, struggling to breathe and sobbing uncontrollably. Linda followed her, placed her arms around the tiny frame and held her until she calmed down and encouraged her to rest.

Amber awoke in the darkness, fully dressed and drained.

'So here I am, an outcast. I'm in a church I don't fit in, a job which I hate, no one calls me and all I want to do is die but I can't because I still have a conscience and I know that I will be killing Jesus as well. He is still in my heart, somewhere in the distance maybe but nevertheless, I know He is here.'

Amber's thoughts to herself were becoming darker and more muddled and she often thought of suicide and became very near on many occasions but this voice inside of her soul stopped her in her tracks. She knew that Linda was right, and she did need professional help. After cleaning her teeth and spraying on some deodorant, picked herself up and plodded down the road to the family she loved very much and they showed her affection. As she rang the bell, which even made her jump, she was welcomed with a smile, and this was to be the first day of the worst time in her life.

She began to open up and poured out her heart to Paul and Jane. It was all mixed up but she felt they understood. They were the only down-to-earth Christians she knew who genuinely cared. She explained how she needed to lose weight, how she had gotten into a trap and couldn't get out.

Somehow, she was desperate for them to wave a magic wand and then she'd be free but that is a devil's trick and a lie. Paul leaned forward and gently told her that she may have anorexia. Though it was gentle, it hit her like a ton of bricks. Struggling to believe his words, gawped at him, dismayed and bewildered. Jane sat next to her on the settee and prayed for peace as the young girl shook.

"Oh, my lover, you're freezing!" exclaimed Jane, who made another cuppa (tea, white with one sugar) together with a hot water bottle for Amber to cuddle.

After a little more persuasion, Amber agreed to make an appointment to see the doctor. Although at the back of her mind she knew that whatever she said to the doctor, he wouldn't believe her as no one else seemed to believe her (including herself if she was totally honest). She convinced herself that she wasn't light enough to be anorexic and hadn't collapsed like the girl on TV, so she must be all right.

"Jump on the scales for me please Amber."

Dr Simms was not only her GP but also a leader at the church she attended, and he was Uncle Jo there.

"Why?" she became defensive.

"Please Amber, it's routine and I'll check your blood pressure too."

She reluctantly stood on the scales knowing that he would advise her to go on a diet as she was positively obese and knew that was the real reason for her feeling unwell.

"6 stone 2lbs," he frowned.

She knew it, too heavy. Maybe he would advise her on how to lose weight, she hoped.

"What is your diet at the moment?" he questioned.

"50 calories a day," she responded.

"So, what is the food you eat?"

"I have one plain Ryvita for breakfast and then half a satsuma for lunch and the other half for tea. I also drink about 10 black coffees to keep me awake. So the total is 50 calories," wondering if a whole Ryvita was too much ….

"Ah, I see."

He peered over the top of his glasses, looking very concerned.

"Am I too fat?" Amber was now feeling sick in the stomach.

"Mmmm, no – that's not the diagnosis sweetheart."

He spoke softly and reassuringly as he could see Amber was looking bewildered and on the verge of tears.

"I would like to refer you to a friend of mine, he is a psychiatrist and specialises in eating disorders. He is a Christian so will understand your faith. I am going to book you in to see him as urgently as possible. You are underweight and if you carry on with that diet young lady you will soon be dead."

He didn't mince his words. Amber was shocked. How on earth could she be underweight? How could he lie to her saying she was skinny when it was clear she was fat? A Christian leader in her church too and she was fond of Uncle Jo, which was very rare for sceptical Amber.

Running home, she made herself sick, took 200 laxatives and cried herself to sleep. She could not see the skin and bones she had become.

This was a nightmare! She was now convinced that they were her enemies, out to ensure she stayed fat. Doctors liked fat people; she knew that. However, she couldn't stand herself if she remained fat, with massive breasts. Desperate to be slim, to get rid of these breasts (which in reality had disappeared into a vest). The whole conversation with her doctor haunted her and succumbed to a state of paranoia – the whole world was out to get her!

She had to be in control of something as her mind was buzzing and going berserk. When she was losing weight, all was calm however if she ever put on weight, even if it was half a pound her day would be ruined.

Her throat was so sore, her neck felt so large and her stomach always ached and stuck out. She was so unbearably conscious about how she looked and had to hide amongst loads of jumpers and loose skirts and baggy dresses so no one could see the fat.

She wanted to exist by herself so she wouldn't hurt those close to her, by her newly developed irritability. She bought herself a little notebook in which she wrote down every tiny thing. The day would be carefully organised and tightly regimented. She wrote down the time to wake up, exercise, what she ate and how many calories per item. She made herself sick, hourly, which was also written down. There were set times when she weighed herself and noted down how much she lost. On top of this, were precise times when laxatives were taken in amounts of 10 lots of 10. Such was her regime that if friends asked her over for tea, she had to refuse because it had not been written down in her little red book.

When she went to the doctor, he wanted to see her each week – she was weighed with her clothes on. She clocked onto this and put on extra jumpers to remain the same weight so he would have no idea. It wasn't until she went to the hospital to see Dr Brown that all was revealed.

Dr Brown was a young man in his late 20s and upon seeing her for the first time, captured the young girl's deceit and saw right through the jumpers.

"Down to your undies please, Amber."

She gasped, she knew that she couldn't fool this man, being an expert in his field.

Standing on the scales, with knickers and a vest (no need for a bra) she held her breath and looked down.

"5 stone 3 pounds" he declared.

"That's interesting, your last weight from Dr Simms said 5 stone 8? I guess he weighed you with clothes, eh?" he winked. Yep he wasn't to be fooled.

He attempted to take blood but couldn't find a vein in her tiny arm. Her arms became all bruised, looking like she had been in a fight after a few tries with the needle.

"This isn't going to be possible," he looked concerned.

"If you go below 5 stone, your life is in danger. I will have no alternative but to admit you to hospital."

She understood the seriousness now and felt utterly out of control. She was convinced that she was in control of her weight, her calorie intake, everything. Despite her head being all over the place, at least she was in control of her body. Until now! She had now hit rock bottom and even struggled to walk feeling extremely weak. As she gazed, as if in a trance, straight at Dr Brown she saw Robert's face instead.

"I told you that your walk with God would not be an easy one. Remember, my girl, you will have extreme dark moments, but none as bad as this one."

It was as if she was back in his lounge, Tracy sitting beside her and Robert holding her hands, recalling her encounter with Jesus the day after attempting suicide on 9th June 1984.

Robert's face changed in front of her and there sat Dr Brown and she screamed!

With her thoughts racing, faster than Concorde – her body started convulsing and shaking vigorously. Dr Brown suddenly banged on the panic button and a whole team of nurses came rushing in to sit on her. The petrified teenager saw them as men leaping from their chairs shouting 'Get out! In the name of Jesus,' as she tried to run away. Flashbacks of a man in black with a large knife mocking her as a tiny girl lay gagged and bound. Dozens of images flooded Amber's head. She had no more energy to scream and fight, a pillow was placed over her head, and she froze as she felt a needle jab into her and died.

Chapter 30

**MUFFLED IN THE DISTANCE WAS
THE SOUND OF A TROLLEY.**

"Hello, my lovely. Would you like a cuppa?"

Amber's eyes flickered with the bright dazzling lights and pulled the duvet over her head feebly.

"I shall take that as a, 'yes please'."

The matron placed the tea on a bed tray and sat next to her.

"You're my last patient of the morning, my sweet. Nice of you to wake up, it's been a while."

Amber peeped through the duvet and saw a plump lady with light brown curly hair, large glasses and a warm smile. She didn't want to say a thing, as she had no idea what had happened or where she was and remained silent.

"Well, my name is Matron Joan, and I will be looking after you for a little bit until you are feeling stronger. You rest, my girl and I'll pop around later with the doctor for a little chat when you are up to it."

Chapter 31

It came to a crunch where God seemed very far away and unreachable. Although in her heart she knew He was on the bed beside her, waiting for her to fall into His arms where He would feed her and comfort her to make her well, whilst there was an inner battle for her soul.

She persisted in going to the church meetings even though they were extremely difficult to listen to, putting her on an emotional roller coaster. She began to journal in order to place her thoughts on paper, maybe someone would read these one day and understand.

"Often God would tell me He loved me, but I felt that I couldn't go to Him in the state I was in and I had to come to terms with the fact that I had somehow backslidden and was on very sandy ground.

I realised that I could go no further without God, and I needed Him more than anyone else, yet I was too scared of more condemnation and I couldn't face it.

Then I heard a sermon about how the devil makes us feel condemned and deceives us into thinking that it is brought on by the judgement of God and we deserve to be tossed to and fro on stormy waters.

But God says, "Come to Me, all who are weary and heavy laden and I will give you rest. Take My yoke upon you and learn of Me for I am lowly and gentle in heart, for My yoke is easy and My burden is light and you will find rest for your soul."

I had listened to the devil so much that I didn't even know who was who. I was confused and bewildered by the reaction inside of me whilst listening to sermons. The contemplation of being released from pain provoked insecurity of an unknown freedom. I had become safe in the familiar hands of bondage. My security was in bondage, being obsessed with food and weight – I was a mess.

The hardest thing now was to let go and to trust my Father in heaven to gently deal with me and set me free. How could I let go? I didn't know how. Talking to people and doctors helped a little but it never solved the problem. I wanted close friends to sort out the problem for me. To somehow pick me up, shake me a lot so all the mess could fly out and hey presto I would be free.

I waited for people to suddenly say something that would make me feel secure. Show me love, so I could then have the confidence to let go. I wanted to know what love was. It seemed a frightening thing to me at the time but if someone showed me what it was, then I could do the same to God.

He would then approve of me and I could then be free. I started to try and work out things in my mind. To organise my feelings into some kind of order so life would be easier. But the more I thought, the more I tried to sort myself out, the harder it became."

Chapter 32

There was news of a young single man joining the church. All the single ladies were intrigued, except for Amber. She had heard, via the grapevine, that he had been in prison for a few years on drug charges in Germany and had been deported back to England to live with his mum.

Richard had spoken to these prisoners about the love of Jesus and how He doesn't condemn but gives us another chance at life. Richard was a faithful member of the congregation, and his heart was full of compassion for everyone, including criminals. He didn't fully fit in with the culture of the church, which was predominantly middle class, coming from cosy protected Christian households. To have an ex-con in the congregation was going to be interesting.

Andrew's life was fully impacted by the visit of Richard in prison and gave his life to Jesus. Amber was now sitting opposite this guy in church. He had a cheesy grin, and dark hair, he had obviously worked out as his muscles protruded out of the tight-fitted shirt he wore. She was suspicious as he beamed a bright smile at her, he could have auditioned for a toothpaste company on TV she thought to herself.

She blushed and looked down, wondering why on earth she would react in such a way, whispering to herself, 'Don't be fooled by him, be careful.'

He was introduced to the congregation by Richard bringing him to the front.

"This is Andrew and the only difference between this man and you is that he was caught!"

Everyone laughed, except Amber. As far as she was concerned, he was a drug trafficker and was responsible for the deaths of drug overdoses and should at least be looking a little guilty for his sins.

How judgemental she had become. Father God reminded her of the verse, "First take the plank out of your own eye, then you can see to take the speck out of your brother's."

She argued in her mind that she had never taken drugs but was reminded by herself of the laxatives and self-harm she had imposed on herself and her rudeness to others.

After the service all the single girls were gathered around him, giggling as if they had never seen a man before. Amber shook her head, as he gave a quick glance in her direction and smiled.

He had barely been in Exeter for a few weeks, and he was already visiting single ladies to help them in their gardens or carry their shopping. He was too helpful and kind for her liking and therefore kept her distance.

She had found a place of her own which was a one-bedroomed flat on the top floor. The landlord was a Christian man but the flats were in desperate need of decoration and modernisation. However, the rent was very cheap, and she was so ready to live on her own as the three girls were becoming unbearably grumpy old spinsters and she didn't want to turn out like them – yep, that's how judgemental she had become. It was probably better that she had her own space.

She was so happy, to venture on her own, no one looking down on her and saying she was too thin. She'd bought paint brushes, rollers and paint (a burgundy colour for the lounge and cream for the bedroom).

Chapter 33

ANDREW

Andrew had heard that a young lady called Amber was decorating and plucked up the courage to ask her if she needed help. He had noticed that she hadn't been as clingy as the other girls, rather quite the opposite, if not a little cold towards him and maybe he could convince her he wasn't all bad and Jesus had really changed his life.

Derek and Christine had been trying for children for 4 years and every year Derek would grumble to his wife.

"Well, that's another 12 disappointments!"

This grieved Christine to the core as she was desperate to have a baby. Watching all her young friends with babies in arms made it all so much harder and the mockery of her new husband was difficult to bear. Christine was a devout Catholic and took her apparent baroness as a form of punishment from God. She entered the confession box daily begging for forgiveness of sins and often wept before the altar at her church, at the foot of the crucifix.

Her prayers were answered, and Christine was thrilled to have given birth to their first baby, Martin. Derek was delighted and celebrated with the lads, over a few pints in the local.

Christine was waiting for her husband to pick her and their baby up from the hospital but heard nothing all day. She had been discharged and waiting in the reception as he was supposed to pick her up at noon and when she called, the phone just rang out. She was beginning to get concerned thinking he may have been involved in a car accident.

However, on the hundredth time of trying, he answered the phone abruptly.

"Woman, I'm busy so you'll have to catch a bus home!"

He hung up! She was fuming!

This was the beginning of quite a turbulent marriage of flaring tempers. Christine was quick-tongued, and Derek was quick-fisted!

With five girls following, Andrew was the final addition to the family and Derek was delighted it was a boy – "One less wedding to pay for," he thought.

The tensions and arguments between Christine and her husband had intensified. So much so, they decided to start afresh in another country with a new business – maybe this would revitalise their marriage and family life.

Moving to New Zealand was seen as a huge adventure for Andrew, at the age of 10 life as the youngest boy he had no worries or cares and adored the outside of the countryside and New Zealand was to prove to be just the best for the young lad.

He had the time of his life, climbing trees, making dens in the woods, and fishing with his mates. His parents and siblings were far too busy working in the hotel they had purchased, to bother about him and his freedom excelled. There were no boundaries, no rules, no older sisters bossing him about – pure bliss.

Andrew was fishing with his mates by the river which flowed at the bottom of his garden. Suddenly he heard a commotion in the kitchen, with what appeared to sound like plates being smashed on the floor. He could hear his father bellowing crossly at his mother, whose response to defend herself was to throw plates at him.

"Bloody woman!" was all they could hear every now and again just after a plate smashed to smithereens.

He and his mates turned around to see his mother running down to the bottom of the garden, hitching her skirt up. She seemed to be heading straight in their direction, screaming.

"He's got a knife!"

Sure enough, there was Derek yielding a kitchen knife chasing her, with his other hand holding a kitchen cloth over his head, ridden with blood. Her aim with the plate, with excellent precision, had succeeded to hit her target.

The next minute, the two lads just stared at her, running straight into the river for protection. Andrew had no idea what got into him, but as his father got closer, he put his foot out and he went head over heels, the knife flying out of his hand and splosh!

Andrew's mate managed to grab the knife from the ground and hid it under the bait tin.

There was a silence and then the pair of them, sopping wet, tempers now drowned, burst out laughing. The gash on his head looked deep, after finding the soaked tea cloth Christine took pity on him, holding it to his wound they both came out of the river.

"Ok love, you win that one!"

"How's the fishing going lads? Caught anything?"

Everyone half chuckled. As Christine was a nurse before having the children, she bandaged up her husband and they carried on cooking the meal for the guests, who were all gawping out of the dining room window during the commotion. They must have thought it was something out of Fawlty Towers!

The fights became more and more intense, and Christine couldn't stand it any longer. She took the youngest two children (Betty and Andrew) with her back to England. She arrived in Wales to start a new life without her troublesome husband, who was always chatting up the girls and didn't take the hotel work seriously at all. She felt that she and the older children were slogging away and he saw his role as entertaining the young ladies. This often culminated in them having atrocious fights and enough was enough when she caught him with his pants down!

This move devastated Andrew. He was 15 years old and being an English/New Zealand lad in Wales became a target for bullying. Unfortunately, he ended up mixing with the wrong crowd and became involved with drug dealing to try and fit in. He had learnt a lot of catering skills working in the kitchen at a hotel in New Zealand and found himself a job in Bournemouth, Dorset. This is where his dealings became serious, with big money and dangerous drug delivery jobs. He was always up for a dare and then came the ultimate challenge.

He was offered a job in a hotel in Amsterdam where Cannabis was legal and he could live life to the full, with no Catholic Mother preaching to him about his need for confession of sins and having to say so many, "Our Fathers" or "Hail Marys" to appease her and God.

Christine was distraught that her baby was running off to Amsterdam, of all places. This is where his life became full of misadventure and mischief. His exuberant personality came to full fruition in Amsterdam, and he enjoyed the freedom of the culture. He was introduced to a Bristol girl, who showed him the ropes as they lived in the red-light district. Andrew soon got used to the routine of drinking and smoking hash during the day and working in the hotel during the evenings with ease.

However, their haphazard lifestyle soon caught up with the couple and money became very tight and their relationship was fraught with arguments. Andrew was stretched out on the couch, can of beer in one hand and preparing a spliff before his night shift. Liz flipped, which was not unusual nowadays.

"You're not earning enough at that hotel job!"

"Hey, Woman! I work loads of hours for tuppence, what do you want, blood!" retorted Andrew.

"Did you hear about Jack? He's just done a job for a local gang that deals with drug trafficking. You'd get more dosh for a few days travelling than two months working at that dive of a hotel."

Andrew didn't take too much persuading to fly to India and back a few times, due to the colossal amount of money he took home.

He had his story all figured out. He was a 'deep sea diver' and had all the equipment, wet suit, flippers and oxygen tanks. The drugs were sealed in between the lining of the empty oxygen tanks and weighed precisely the same amount as oxygen-filled cylinders. Everything was handed to him by the top gang members with a reward of a free hotel stay and cash in hand, lots of cash.

On his third trip, he went through as normal – as they were metal canisters they couldn't be detected as harbouring cannabis.

Everything was going to plan until he got off the plane to collect his luggage and diving equipment. He was still waiting for the luggage and when the last one was picked up, he was left gawping at an empty conveyor belt. The security guard was watching him closely, Andrew turned around and two more officers were chatting, and he was convinced something was going on. He put on his 'keeping cool appearance' and walked to the information desk with a swagger.

"Could you check for my luggage, it's not arrived and I need it urgently for a dive tomorrow first thing."

"So sorry Sir, can I have your details and we will investigate for you?"

He was aware that the security guard was keeping his eye on him, the two other officers were also watching him now.

"Could you wait for a few minutes Sir, there appears to be a problem?"

Becoming irate with them, realising his keeping cool act was wavering by nerves.

"I'm shattered and I've got a dive first thing. This is the name of my hotel, please call the number when it has been found."

"Ah ok, Sir. Thank you, we will notify you and understand its importance."

Catching the taxi, he arrived at the hotel with his heart pumping ferociously and needed a couple of drinks to calm himself down. The clock was ticking away and it had been a couple of hours and becoming quite late. He was due to drop the equipment off first thing in the morning, so what was he to say?

The phone rang in his room, they put the call through to him from the Airport.

"Hello, Mr Jackson – we have retrieved your luggage as it was mistakenly put onto the wrong aircraft. However, there seems to be a problem with it. Please could you come to the Airport to sign for the luggage with some documents for the equipment, Sir?"

"No way, I'm shattered it's your fault that it had been mislaid, get someone to bring my equipment here to the hotel and I will show you the documents and sign for it here."

Slamming the phone down, he paced up and down, panicking. What kind of problem? His mind racing, does he run now, does he hang in there – have they seen what has been hidden? Being caught in Germany, whilst in transit was not good news at all.

About half an hour later the phone rings again.

"Your luggage is here, Sir", said the receptionist.

He went downstairs looking cross, "Where do you want me to sign?"

He signed the papers and grabbed his equipment and luggage. The young courier was too scared to ask for the documents to prove the validity of the diving equipment as instructed and sped off.

Andrew didn't breathe normally until he got to his room and boy was he relieved when the deal when through and the cash was in his hand.

'That was a close one ... that could be the last as well, as not sure it's worth the stress,' he muttered to himself.

The money soon got spent. One of the team got caught with the drugs in the oxygen tanks so that story will have to change. However, they had a large order of 64kg of cannabis that needed to be shipped from India to Amsterdam.

So, he was enticed with more money to use a plain suitcase, packed full. He was reluctant as he had convinced himself he was a deep-sea diver and that story worked a treat for him. This was a far greater risk.

Once at the airport, he had his suitcase weighed, going through security was easy, too easy. Sitting in the waiting room at the airport for his plane, just half an hour to go so he was almost there. Looking across he noticed a gentleman in a dark grey suit peering at him over the top of his newspaper. Was he beginning to feel the paranoia? To be sure, he went to the toilet and from the corner of his eye, saw him get up and follow him. Just a coincidence, he pondered. Boarding time, on the plane and very relieved, closed his eyes for the journey.

He was familiar with the transit flight in Frankfurt, as this was the fourth time around and he had passed through the hardest part of the journey now.

Two policemen came charging through the aircraft, "Mr Jackson?"

He looked up, shaking his head, however, the officers ignored him, abruptly grabbed his wrist and 'clunk' on went the handcuffs connected to one of the officers.

"You've got the wrong guy; this is a mistake!" shouting and bawling as he was forced off the plane with everyone just gawping at him.

He was found guilty and served 4 years of a 6-year sentence. Here he was now back in his hometown of Exeter living with his mother. After his newfound faith, he wanted to find a girl, get married, have children and settle down – he was getting older now being 28. He had introduced himself to most of the girls at the church, except Amber. He needed to check them all out before making up his mind about which one to marry.

She was younger than the others and there was something about her. She was constantly on his mind – then he heard via one of the elders at the church that she needed help in decorating. Now, was his chance – she appeared to be quite off with him and when he smiled, she just glared and turned away.

This wasn't going to be as easy as the others, he pondered, but it was worth a try.

Chapter 34

Amber had been chatting to Tim, one of the elders about decorating her bedroom. She had done the lounge and just wanted it all finished now.

"How about asking Andrew?" suggested Tim.

"Ah Nah!" she retorted.

"Why not?"

"He's a criminal, drug dealer – he is guilty of killing many people who've taken his stuff and I don't trust him." She was cross with Tim for suggesting such a thing, hadn't he seen behind the smile and charm?

"Amber, he WAS a criminal, his life has been turned around and he wants to make a fresh start. Jesus has forgiven his sins, just the same as you. Maybe you need to stop being so judgemental in your attitude and give him a second chance too?" quizzed Tim.

She went away feeling rebuked, she was very fond of Tim and respected him as one of the elders at the church. After pondering and repeatedly hearing in her head, 'Stop being so judgemental' – she knew in her heart that she also needed to change. Her bedroom did need decorating, so she agreed.

Andrew couldn't believe it. She actually said, 'Yes' to decorating the bedroom, but you never know, one step at a time with this one.

He bought some new paintbrushes and a roller and tray. She had bought the paint and all he had to do was impress her and was sure he could swipe her off her feet. He rang the doorbell and she opened the door, her brunette hair tied up in a ponytail, dungarees and a bright pink T-shirt. She had the most beautiful figure, even in dungarees.

"Come on in Andrew and thank you for helping me out."

She put on her best behaviour and decided to give him a chance but to be guarded. She had noticed he had dazzling hazel eyes, with this olive complexion and muscles, he was handsome, she had to admit. Realising her thoughts, stopped herself … 'Remember to be guarded.' ….

He was a little more nervous than she had envisaged. He had come across as overconfident, even too exuberant, whilst in public at church. He stumbled his words slightly and appeared bashful. She couldn't believe that she had to put him at ease so yep, she had maybe judged him too harshly, as she did.

A quick cuppa and they both started decorating the bedroom. As soon as he got to work, he relaxed, and they chatted very amicably. Time went so quickly and he sure was a dab hand with the paintbrush, it was a lot more fun decorating the room with some company and she had to admit deep down she enjoyed his company.

"Well, that's one coat finished. How about I come back after church tomorrow and we could do the second coat?" he quizzed.

"That's a good idea, how many coats does it need?"

"Oh, quite a few, I reckon!" he smiled and winked at the same time. They both burst out laughing.

He was fully relaxed now; he certainly had the charm and he certainly spent quite a bit of time working out by the looks of the muscles protruding from his rather too-small T-shirt.

"See you tomorrow, Amber!"

"I'll make lunch so we can eat after the service and crack on with the second coat," she replied.

As he departed, she closed the door behind her, she felt a deep warm feeling inside, and a smile welled up as she dreamed about his hazel eyes.

So much for being guarded!

Four coats later, he asked her if she'd like to go to a concert. Her first date with just one guy would be good. Her previous experience with dating 3 guys was disastrous and far too complicated.

He didn't say what kind of concert it was. The only ones she had been to in the past were classical concerts with her dad. This was at the university campus, so she assumed it would be similar. She came straight from work in her black pencil skirt, white blouse and heels so didn't need to change as was smart enough for a concert.

Andrew, however, was dressed very casually in a bright yellow T-shirt with a 12-pointed star and a Rastafarian symbol and jeans. She immediately thought, 'he's so underdressed for a concert' and felt embarrassed for him but didn't say anything.

There was a bouncer at the door and many young people, also casually dressed crowded around the entrance. She assumed that they were going to a gig or something and not the same concert they were going to.

He grabbed hold of her hand, and his eyes were misty this time, not clear hazel as before. They barged through the crowd and entered a massive hall. Jam packed full of people, there were no chairs, no orchestra. The air was thick with the smell of incense.

"What kind of concert is this?" she gasped.

"Gregory Isaacs!" he exclaimed and by now with the first bands playing he was out of it – dancing weirdly.

Embarrassed with people staring at her, she took off her shoes, wrapped her cardy around her middle and joined in. The incense was now potent and she became quite chilled.

Gregory Isaacs didn't come on stage until 11 pm and it finished at 2 am. Exhausted and in bed for 4 am, it wasn't quite what she expected – good job it was Friday night so she could have a lie in.

She was invited to lunch with Uncle Paul and Jane, which had been arranged so they could keep an eye on her. They were not impressed with a Reggae concert and 'incense'.

"Mmmm, so he doesn't do drugs anymore then?" asked Jane.

"Nop, just incense," she chuckled.

The couple looked concerned, shaking their heads simultaneously.

"Oh, Amber please be careful. Don't let your heart get before sense?" warned Uncle Paul.

However, they both felt it had already happened, as she giggled constantly like a schoolgirl.

They prayed for her, to use wisdom and for Father God to direct her paths.

Andrew noticed that when they met for coffee, she didn't eat anything. Whenever he suggested they went out for a meal, she would decline. He had come out of prison with a limited diet and every time he passed a cake shop, he couldn't resist the luscious chocolate cream eclairs or the large jam doughnuts. His six-pack was turning into a blob of fat and he was not happy. Amber had recently joined a gym, was very keen on sport and seemed to spend quite a bit of time there. So, instead of going out for meals, they both met to play squash, badminton, swimming, jogging and cycling.

For Amber, this was a healthy distraction as she was keen to keep the weight off. Her appointments with the psychiatrist were now reduced to biweekly as he could see a glimpse of progression as Amber's conversation became very much centred on her newfound boyfriend than food. This was a healthy sign and he could see that she was beginning to relax and even smile.

Andrew and Amber's relationship blossomed. He soon realised that she had an unhealthy obsession with calories and she was unbearably thin. She took forever to eat her lunch (one fat-free yoghurt) a total of 50 calories, she pointed out to him. When he came around for coffee, he would prepare her yoghurt in a small bowl and secretly put in some bodybuilders' powder, to the value of 500 calories. Little did she know that when she put in her little book – one yoghurt of 50 calories it would have been 550.

They had been dating now for 6 weeks, and all her doubts at the beginning had been completely forgotten. Sitting by the canal, in the gorgeous sunshine, the bees buzzing around the dandelions, he knew this was the perfect moment to formally ask her out.

Staring into each other's eyes, transfixed by each other, his heart pumping ten to the dozen, hoping he hadn't rushed things too much. She was smiling the most beaming smile, and noticed a twinkle in his eye, turning her head to one side.

"What are you thinking?" she quizzed.

"Would you like to go out with me, as in being my girlfriend?" he stuttered.

It sounded so pathetic, he just didn't know how or what to say, suddenly his speech became impaired and he felt so embarrassed as she was silent.

Amber was never one for waiting or taking things slowly. She did tend to be very spontaneous which was often her downfall but sometimes so much fun!

"I'd love to be your girlfriend, however, ..." she hesitated, ... "as a Christian, I don't want to be going out with you for anything other than marriage."

Delighted he quickly responded, "Will you marry me then?"

"Yes, I will!" she exclaimed.

He grabbed hold of her and spun her around very excitedly. "You really mean it!"

She was so excited she called Paul and Jane straight away. They were not as keen as she was and seemed quite apprehensive. It's very quick Amber, you've only known each other for 6 weeks. There was no stopping Amber when she had an idea. 'It was all or nothing with her,' they said to one another.

They became engaged on her 21st birthday with a date for marriage on 3rd February 1990, six months to prepare.

The time went very quickly – they didn't have much money between them. They decided to have a small wedding with 50 guests and arranged for a family business to do the reception meal. It was to be vegetarian and no alcohol, as it was on the church premises.

Amber's work colleague had been married a few months before and lent her, her wedding dress as money was tight and it was just for a day. They were about the same size; the dress had a 19-inch waist so fitted her perfectly. Their friends had a very nice Volvo, upon which they tied a pale pink ribbon, to dress it up as the car to take the bride to the church. She wasn't sure if her dad was going to make it, but she did ring him the day before to check. His response was typical.

"What's happening tomorrow? – I'll have to check my diary and I may come but then again, I may not!" he abruptly put the phone down.

She wasn't that bothered; their relationship had been fractious and quite distant since she left home. She therefore arranged for a backup dad, just in case, to walk her up the aisle.

She went to Uncle Paul and Jane's house on the morning of the wedding. Jane helped Amber get into her wedding dress. It was made of white lace with a pink ribbon around the waist.

Jane started to laugh, "Oh Amber, I can't see your eyes, your fringe is too long. Let me cut it."

She found the scissors and carefully put a piece of paper under her chin so the hair wouldn't get onto the gorgeous white dress.

"Perfect, I can see you now!" and they both giggled.

Then the doorbell rang, and Jane went to answer it – "Oh hello?"

To her surprise, her dad was standing there, very nervous. Amber was quietly pleased that he had turned up to walk her down the aisle.

So, here she was – the music playing, arm in arm with her dad, who was whispering, "This is the worst day of my life."

She ignored him as they were walking down the aisle. This was HER day, and he wasn't going to destroy this for her. She was beaming and radiant as her man was waiting for her at the front.

Andrew couldn't take his eyes off her. She was beautiful and with her petite frame the gorgeous white lacy dress made her look like a porcelain doll – so delicate and he adored her.

A man who professed to love her, to hold her and to keep her safe. This was the start of her new life, to start again and enjoy life, for real.

The minister smiled at them both.

"Andrew, do you take this woman to be your wife, to live together in holy matrimony, to love her, to honour her, to comfort her and to keep her in sickness and in health, forsaking all others, for as long as you both shall live?"

Printed and bound by CPI Group (UK) Ltd, Croydon, CR0 4YY